GAY SCIENCE

GAY SCIENCE

THE *TOTALLY SCIENTIFIC* EXAMINATION OF
LGBTQ+ CULTURE, MYTHS, **AND** STEREOTYPES

ROB ANDERSON

Publisher Mike Sanders
Senior Editor Alexander Rigby
Editorial Director Ann Barton
Art & Design Director William Thomas
Designer Joanna Price
Photographer Noah Fecks
Photo Researcher Micah Schmidt
Copy Editor Devon Fredericksen
Proofreaders Lisa Starnes, Claire Safran
Sensitivity Readers Drew Hubbard, Ava Mortier
Indexer Celia McCoy

First American Edition, 2024
Published in the United States by DK Publishing
1745 Broadway, 20th Floor, New York, NY 10019

The authorized representative in the EEA is Dorling
Kindersley Verlag GmbH. Arnulfstr. 124, 80636
Munich, Germany

Library of Congress Catalog Number: 2023947874
ISBN: 978-0-7440-8735-2

DK books are available at
special discounts when purchased
in bulk for sales promotions, premiums,
fund-raising, or educational use. For details,
contact SpecialSales@dk.com

Printed and bound in China

www.dk.com

This book was made with Forest
Stewardship Council™ certified
paper – one small step in DK's
commitment to a sustainable future.
Learn more at
www.dk.com/uk/information/sustainability

BEFORE YOU BAN THIS BOOK

We aren't sure where you found *Gay Science*, but your choice to open it up is a total slay. (We won't say "slay" again but we had to get it out of our system.)

Inside you'll find important coursework in continuing adult education. Though the material is very scientific in every kind of real way, it is not intended for children. If you think it might be for kids, then you're probably really dumb.

If you grabbed this book with the hope of indoctrinating minors, you're out of luck. But kids will believe anything you tell them, so we'd be happy to suggest other texts that have proven to be quite good at that sort of thing:

The Holy Bible
The Gita
The Torah
The Qur'an
The Book of Mormon
Dianetics

Don't Say We Didn't Say This

I believe that a good joke is one that not everyone will get, and if you twist yourself in knots to make sure everyone understands it, you've probably already ruined it. So I don't like to do that.

But my publisher is making me add this page because though they're fully obsessed with *Gay Science*, they do produce real educational books, and they're worried people will take this seriously. Even though I'm holding an enema as a pipette on the cover.

So I'll say this once: this is satire. I did not create the queer stereotypes in this book. A few of these generalizations were made in ignorance by bigoted people over the years, while the rest were created with a sillier intent by the LGBTQ+ community itself. We're about to have fun with all of them.

Trigger Warning: ~~This book uses~~ reclaimed words like "fag" and "dyke." It also uses the name "James Corden," and honestly I think that's much more derogatory. I stand by everything I've written, unless you don't think it's funny. Then I better start preparing my notes apology.

Rob Arden

Dedicated to the girls, gays, and theys.

Table of Contents

What Is Gay Science?

Let's say you're anything but straight. Like Christmas trees ripped from a farm, every December you are forced to leave a comfortable habitat to sit in a living room with a heterosexual family in the suburbs. This is called visiting family, and it's not technically a hate crime, but it sure feels like one. You need a break from this indentured servitude, so you meet up with some high school friends to look at old yearbooks together. You notice something. Everyone else seems to look much worse now than they did back then, but you're significantly hotter. If you're all the same age, why don't you look like them? Why did they age like they grabbed the wrong Holy Grail cup in *Indiana Jones* and you're preserved all nicely like a fierce mosquito stuck in amber? This is Gay Science.

Or maybe you're running fifteen minutes late to work because you were lying in bed, playing out a fabricated scenario in your head that you'll never actually encounter. You're not worried because you're gay and walking to work. You enjoy the natural high of speeding past slow straight people and sit at your desk at a cute five minutes past. Did you just defy the laws of physics? This is also Gay Science.

Or maybe you're trying to get revenge on your ex-boyfriend, so you enlist your stepbrother to seduce your ex's current girlfriend. But his girlfriend falls in love with her music teacher, and after a series of lies, blackmailing, and underage alcohol consumption, your stepbrother is hit by a car and tragically dies. This is not Gay Science. It's the plot of *Cruel Intentions*. But Sarah Michelle Gellar hiding cocaine in a crucifix? That's so Gay Science.

In this groundbreaking, probably already-banned book for adults, you'll explore 3 branches and 29 fields of Gay Science. You'll learn about the subspecies of DIY lesbians, how to diagnose bisexual panic, why gay men feel powerful immediately after a haircut, and all the LGBTQ+ things they left out of your standard science curriculum. There are even some experiments you can try at home!

Words or phrases in orange can be found in The Gloss: our gay glossary that defines terms, explains references, and notes some of the "real" science behind what you're reading. The Gloss starts on page 223.

The Gay Scientific Method

Critical Thinking

Queer people are excellent critical thinkers! From a very young age they have been conditioned to seek solutions for problems that other people have created for them. This problem-solving quality is the basis of the **gay scientific method**: an alternate (and fruity) form of determining what's real in our world. On the left you'll find the boring way to draw scientific conclusions.

On the right, Gay Science, which doesn't have the time for all that because it's, like, really busy. Let's find a shortcut! Because our science is gay, it puts you in the center of the universe. Your personal experiences are now irrefutable facts!

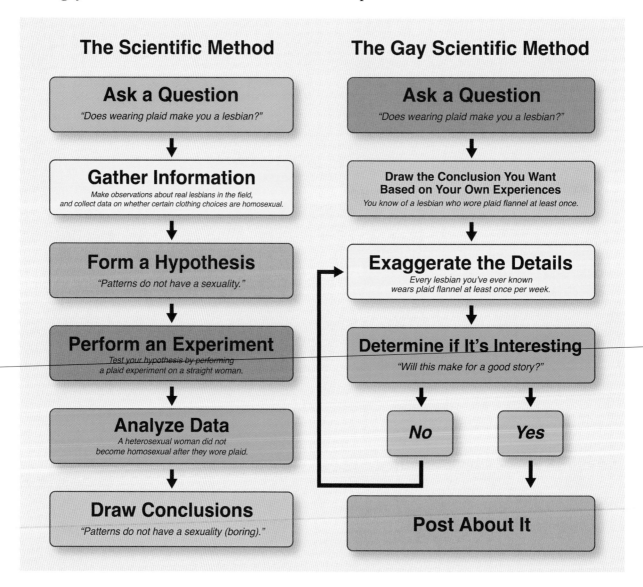

The Scientific Method

Ask a Question
"Does wearing plaid make you a lesbian?"

↓

Gather Information
Make observations about real lesbians in the field, and collect data on whether certain clothing choices are homosexual.

↓

Form a Hypothesis
"Patterns do not have a sexuality."

↓

Perform an Experiment
Test your hypothesis by performing a plaid experiment on a straight woman.

↓

Analyze Data
A heterosexual woman did not become homosexual after they wore plaid.

↓

Draw Conclusions
"Patterns do not have a sexuality (boring)."

The Gay Scientific Method

Ask a Question
"Does wearing plaid make you a lesbian?"

↓

Draw the Conclusion You Want Based on Your Own Experiences
You know of a lesbian who wore plaid flannel at least once.

↓

Exaggerate the Details
Every lesbian you've ever known wears plaid flannel at least once per week.

↓

Determine if It's Interesting
"Will this make for a good story?"

No   *Yes*

Post About It

PART 1

Natural Sciences

This branch of science helps us understand the massively homosexual world around us. While traditional natural sciences use data and peer review to determine what's real, gay natural sciences use vibes and what people say on the internet to draw final conclusions. These upcoming fields of science will tackle all the gay things we can see and feel (with consent!).

Biology
Take a look inside the gay cell.

Anatomy
Understand how gay bodies work and why size really does matter.

Pathology
Learn how to keep your body healthy from LGBTQ+ viruses, bacteria, and other diseases like the state of Florida.

Microbiology
Let Gay Science explain why lesbians don't have technology in their love stories.

Physics
Understand nonliving gay systems, like the gravitational pull of gray sweatpants.

Chemistry
Learn about the strongest bond known to man: the one between the girls and the gays.

Geology
Gaydar goes much deeper than intuition. Literally into the earth's crust.

Oceanography
Gay friend groups are like ocean currents, always changing but highly predictable.

Genetics
Dominant and recessive traits help you understand if the other gay is friend or foe.

Nutrition
Cold coffee isn't just a gay preference, it's a critical nutrient.

Botany
We unpack why the Plant Gay is one of the most fascinating subtypes of homosexual.

Zoology
Examine how gay men transition one-off sexual encounters into besties with the Hookup-to-Friends Metamorphosis.

Ecology
Camp? So gay. Camping? Not so much.

Astronomy
Are there signs of queer life in outer space? Duh, babe.

Biological Classification

The Tea: If you don't know how to label yourself, how in the hell are you going to label someone else?

Get PrEPared

You'll learn how to:
✔ **Classify** people by category
✔ **Determine** what kind of box you fit into

Why it's important:
✔ Stereotyping yourself first (before someone else does) is one way to own your power.

The three-toed sloth belongs to the Bradypodidae family and leaves us completely emotionally destroyed.

We All Belong in Categories!

A sloth and an anteater look kinda similar, don't they? They have a lot in common: (1) You can find them in South America, (2) They live in trees, and (3) Looking at them just makes you want to sob. Just like full-on bawling for hours.

But they also have their differences! (1) They have different-sized heads, (2) They don't have the same diet, (3) The sloth makes us cry because we want to be friends, but the anteater makes us cry because we want it to live forever!

This is because even though they share the same order (*Pilosa*), they belong to different *families*. Science categorizes all living beings with this taxonomy, but Gay Science puts queer people in a system of its own.

The silky anteater belongs to the Cyclopedidae family and makes us wonder if we'll ever be the same again.

The Sass-onomic Pyramid

LGBTQ+ people are sorted into a five-part classification system.

If we didn't categorize groups of people by their immediately identifiable traits, we wouldn't be able to function. Without labels, our community could sink into chaos, though lesbians would never let that happen (but more on that later). LGBTQ+ people live and die by their classifications. It's who they are. We call this ranking system the **sass-onomic pyramid**.

UMBRELLA
Example: LGBTQ+
This is any human being that has claimed LGBTQ+ status. And witches.

LETTER
Example: Lesbian (L)
This is the self-assigned individual letter identity. If an LGBTQ+ believes they may belong to multiple letters, they have to choose their fave (for now).

TYPE
Example: Butch
This is usually related to their outward appearance. How would you label this person just by looking at them?

SUBTYPE
Example: Lumberjack/Lumbersexual
What kind of flavor would they be?

SUB-SUBTYPE
Example: Environmentally Sustainable
This is usually related to their actions, behaviors, and hobbies.

The name is read from the bottom up. So this would be an environmentally sustainable, lumberjack butch lesbian.

Lesbian Classification

To further categorize themselves, the LGBTQ+ use **bi-binomial nomenclature**. Lesbians give themselves a four-part name in this order: the sub-subtype, subtype, type, and letter.

LESBIAN BI-BINOMIAL NOMENCLATURE

Sub-subtype	Subtype	Type	Letter
	Business		
	Solar		
	Nuclear	Power	
	Horse		
	Flower		
Rosetta			
Blarney			
Grave	Stone	Butch	
Stoned (weed)			
Memory Foam			
Feather Down	Pillow Princess	Femme	
Feather Down Alternative			Lesbian
Balm			
Stick	Carmex		
		Chapstick	
SPF 15			
SPF 30	Blistex		
Demolition			
Roller	Derby		
Kentucky			
		Sporty	
Soft			
Basket	Ball		
Meat			
Raw			
Fake	Vegan	Cottagecore	

Gay Classification

For gay men, all the types are interchangeable. Start with the letter (Gay) and move downward to the sub-subtype, then the subtype, followed by the type.

GAY BI-BINOMIAL NOMENCLATURE

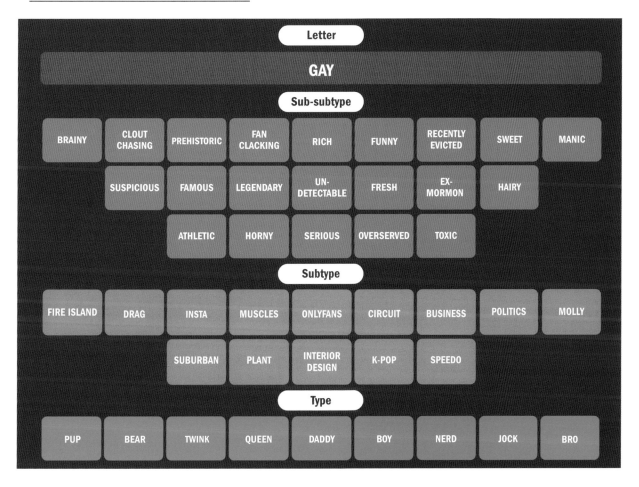

A HOMOSEXUAL CLASSIFYING ANOTHER:

"That is a gay fan-clacking muscle pup."

Serving Conclusions

→ Gay people love to make things up.

→ Sloths and anteaters make us cry.

→ Fake vegan cottagecore lesbians do exist.

Why Do Gays Love Drama?

The Tea: The girls (who we don't know) are fighting! (We heard.)

Get PrEPared

You'll learn how to:
- ✔ **Identify** the parts of a gay cell
- ✔ **Compare** different types of gay drama

Why it's important:
- ✔ Gay men live on unverified information.

Where There's Drama . . .

. . . there's usually a gay around. They manage the remarkable achievement of shaping the narrative surrounding others' business without any direct involvement in the drama. A gay will know that the company CFO is cheating on his wife before she does . . . and they don't even work at that company.

After selectively amplifying certain aspects of the story for jaw-dropping impact, the gay knows when to disengage from the gossip and focus on their own affairs, thus sidestepping any entanglements or conflicts.

How do they have the time to consume every Bravo reality TV show and their spin-offs? How are they able to break down the recent **makeup influencer drama** in under one minute? How do they balance their television, parasocial, and real-life drama? Gays are merely responding to a natural biological drive.

A Gay Cell

Our cells need to eat to survive. Animal cells bring in water, oxygen, sodium, and potassium. Plant cells convert carbon dioxide and light energy into glucose and oxygen. A gay cell is fed with an entirely different set of nutrients: drama! First, let's look at the gay cell.

Homosexual males gossiping about who took loads this weekend.

GAY CELL CROSS SECTION

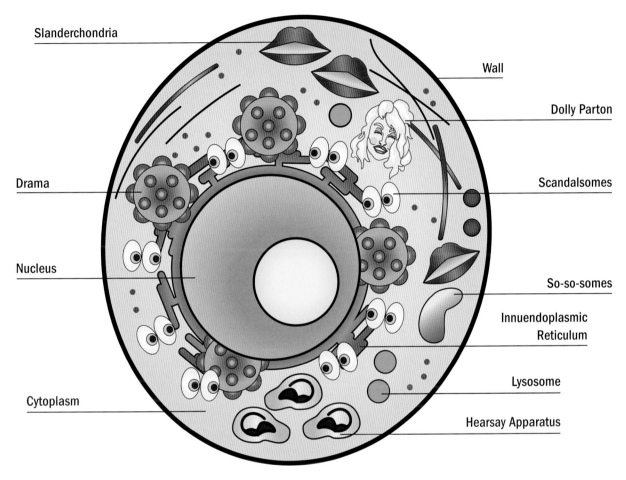

Slanderchondria

Wall

Dolly Parton

Drama

Scandalsomes

Nucleus

So-so-somes

Innuendoplasmic Reticulum

Cytoplasm

Lysosome

Hearsay Apparatus

Gay Nutrition: Drama

Wall

The outside of the gay cell is lined with **gossipids**, which have dramaphilic (drama-loving) heads and repercussionphobic (consequence-fearing) tails. These ensure the retention of drama while preventing any adverse consequences of direct involvement.

Once inside, the drama is sorted into different parts of the cell.

Innuendoplasmic Reticulum

The **innuendoplasmic reticulum** can either be sub (smooth) or dom (rough). The smooth type detoxifies the drama, removing any details that may negatively impact them or a bestie. The rough type does quality control, making sure we're dealing with the fun kind of drama and not the kind that will leave the gay depressed.

Scandalsomes

The **scandalsomes** store the blueprints for every variety of drama within the cell and categorize them accordingly. This is how a gay can assimilate and organize different types of drama all at once!

Nucleus

All new drama is packed and stored permanently inside the **gay nucleus**. This part of the cell can recall specific details about the personal lives of strangers and fictional characters. It might know which housewife had a bow eaten off their cake (Heather), but it won't remember the birthdays of close relatives.

Slanderchondria

The sorted drama moves to the **slanderchondria**, which determines how much slander the gay will add to the situation. It examines the relationship between the drama and the gay, as well as what kind of slander has already been said. If the gay maintains equal relationships with everyone involved, there may be little to no disparagement. However, if there's already been a pile on, the gay may rake the offender over the hot coals. Full-blown defamation.

Hearsay Apparatus

The **hearsay apparatus** determines how long the drama should stay in the cell. Some drama can feed a homosexual for months or years, while less interesting news is in and out in a day.

So-so-somes

The **so-so-somes** break down so-so or worn-out drama that's been lingering too long.

Drama

Though technically not part of the cell, it fuels it.

Cytoplasm

Cytoplasm does absolutely nothing productive for the cell, but it used to date a scandalsome, so now it's kinda stuck here.

Dolly Parton

The spirit of **Dolly Parton** lives in every cell of every gay person, though she is not involved in processing the drama.

Animal cells use passive and active transport to bring in the molecules the body needs. A gay cell has its own versions: **pasivo and activo** transport.

Pasivo Transport

This is a passive process where light drama flows freely in and out of the cell without using much energy. Some examples are:

- **Emmy snubs**
- **Getting in the wrong Uber**
- **Reading about an influencer getting canceled**
- **Misgendering someone's dog**

Activo Transport

This is an active process that requires energy to move large pieces of drama in and out of the cell. This is heavier drama like:

- **Oscar snubs**
- **Any Internet exchanges between Kim Cattrall and Sarah Jessica Parker**
- **Daniel from IT sucking your boss's dick at the company crab boil**
- **Being caught in a lesbian love triangle**

A dog who has no idea you just misgendered them.

The company crab boil of 2018.
Not pictured: Daniel from IT and your boss.

DOLLY PARTON SAYS:

"I love you and I'm always here for you, but keep me out of your lesbian love triangle."

Serving Conclusions

→ Gays stir the pot then leave it to boil over.

→ Oscar snubs > Emmy snubs.

→ Cytoplasm, what are you even doing here?

Power Lesbians, the Stem Cells of the LGBTQ+

The Tea: If you want something done right, get a power lesbian to do it.

Get PrEPared

You'll learn how to:

✔ **Compare** a stem cell and a power lesbian

✔ **Understand** Power lesbian skills

Why it's important:

✔ A power lesbian could probably get you out of jail or something.

The Human Body Is So LGBTQ+

The human body can do amazing things, like appreciate how snatched you look in the corner of your phone screen while simultaneously console a friend on FaceTime. Different types of cells work together in our bodies to help us accomplish these extraordinary things, each with their own specific purpose.

The LGBTQ+ Umbrella works in the same way! Let's take a look at different letters and types within the LGBTQ+ Parasol and see what cells they represent.

Golden retriever lesbians are the *hepatocytes*, or the liver cells, of the LGBTQ+. Rarely in a bad mood, these hypersweet gay women avoid negativity and have a detoxifying effect.

Trans people are the community's *myocytes*. They begin their lives as one type of cell but eventually become a different version of those muscle fibers.

New York gays are the *macrophages*, or white blood cells, protecting and repairing those they know well, while treating unfamiliar entities as the enemy. Slightly unpredictable, these cells can sometimes distrust things at random.

Asexuals are the *neurons*, or nerve cells. They do not divide frequently, and are highly active in transmitting clear signals.

What Are Stem Cells?

The human body does have its limits. Bone cells can't behave like skin cells, and skin cells can't do the job of brain cells, and even the brain cells can't predict who a New York Gay will decide to trust.

Stem cells are a bit different and can step in and behave like any of the others. These shape-shifters are always all like, "Just let me do it." The stem cells can't help that they're good at everything.

Power lesbians take the role of stem cells of the LGBTQ+ Raincoat.

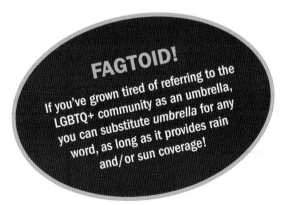

FAGTOID!

If you've grown tired of referring to the LGBTQ+ community as an umbrella, you can substitute *umbrella* for any word, as long as it provides rain and/or sun coverage!

A Power Lesbian Can Do It All

A power lesbian can manage a media empire, work out seven days a week, get reelected to a political office they weren't even holding, impress an entire boardroom of businesspeople, fix a flat, and then make their girlfriend cum so hard it could possibly kill her.

Like stem cells, there are multiple important qualities of a power lesbian:

Les-chastic Differentiation

This occurs when one power lesbian takes a novice under her wing to make her a new power lesbian. While other species in the animal kingdom become weaker from this transfer, the power lesbian remains strong. Her power often becomes even greater from this transfer of energy.

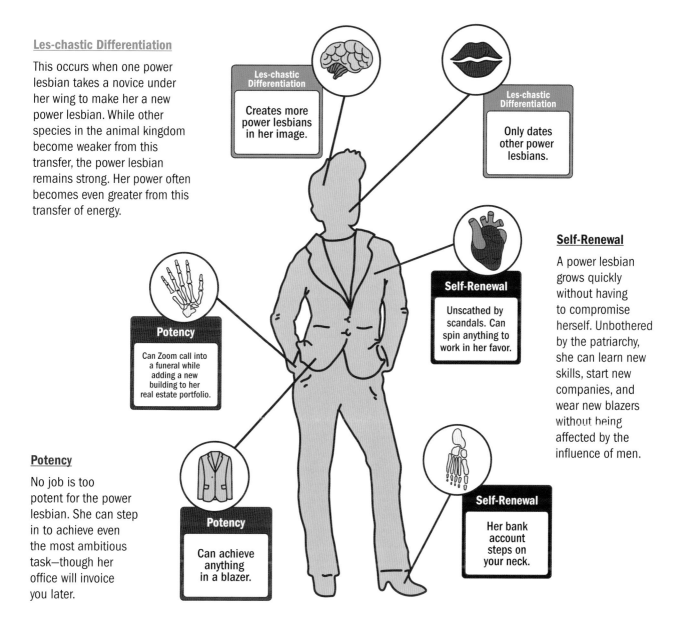

Les-chastic Differentiation

Creates more power lesbians in her image.

Les-chastic Differentiation

Only dates other power lesbians.

Potency

Can Zoom call into a funeral while adding a new building to her real estate portfolio.

Potency

Can achieve anything in a blazer.

Self-Renewal

Unscathed by scandals. Can spin anything to work in her favor.

Self-Renewal

Her bank account steps on your neck.

Potency

No job is too potent for the power lesbian. She can step in to achieve even the most ambitious task—though her office will invoice you later.

Self-Renewal

A power lesbian grows quickly without having to compromise herself. Unbothered by the patriarchy, she can learn new skills, start new companies, and wear new blazers without being affected by the influence of men.

How Powerful Is a Power Lesbian?

Science has yet to determine exactly how much power can be held and unleashed (for more on how lesbians conduct electricity, head to page 50), but some scientists theorize that power lesbians use a very small amount of their available power. This is a mark of their social intelligence as they work to avoid being seen as a threat.

Skill	Yoga Instructor	Man in Finance	The Pope	Power Lesbian
Reading the room	✔	✘	✘	✔
Making money	✘	✔	✔	✔
Showing empathy	✔	✘	✔	✔
Having good taste	✔	✘	✘	✔
Fixing a leak	✘	✘	✘	✔
Playing three instruments	✘	✘	✘	✔
Understanding the art market	✘	✔	✘	✔
Landing a plane	✘	✘	✘	✔
Performing CPR	✘	✘	✘	✔
Winning Jeopardy	✘	✘	✘	✔
Knowing five languages	✘	✘	✔	✔
Knowing ten languages	✘	✘	✘	✔
Getting up early	✔	✔	✘	✔
Staying up late	✘	✔	✘	✔
Staying up late without using cocaine	✘	✘	✘	✔
Easily winning at poker	✘	✔	✘	✔
Losing on purpose at poker to foster a better relationship	✘	✘	✘	✔
Surviving a disaster movie plot	✘	✘	✘	✔
Possessing the palate to taste the difference between every piece of fish during a 15-course omakase	✘	✘	✘	✔

Debunking Power Lesbian Myths

Because power lesbians do not serve the patriarchy, men have created narratives to weaken their influence in society. These are common untruths that have been debunked by the **Jennifer Pritzker Conservatory for Sapphic Habits**.

Yas! OR **NAUR**
(true)   (false)

Power lesbians are responsible for the bee colony collapse.

The bees are dying because many of them live in conservative states, and they really just can't deal anymore.

Power lesbians run the world and all its operations.

Power lesbians do run the world and its operations, but only in secret.

Too many power lesbians in one area can cause an earthquake.

It only takes one power lesbian to initiate an earthquake at any time, but they always choose not to.

Miranda Hobbes is a power lesbian.

Miranda Hobbes is a power bisexual. Cynthia Nixon is a power lesbian.

A Power Bottom Explains

POWER LESBIANS

It's about control. You're in charge, babe. You're defying what's expected of your position, taking back centuries of domination and oppression. You might be 5'6" and weigh 130 pounds, but you're the boss and you'll make him—

Wait, this is about power *lesbians*? Oh, I don't know any of those.

Serving Conclusions

→ **Power lesbians create new power lesbians, then date them.**

→ **A power lesbian can outpower the pope.**

→ **Sorry you got dumped, but I'm looking good in that front-facing camera.**

Why Are Gay Men Terrible Drivers?

The Tea: But they're great at using Apple CarPlay.

Get PrEPared

You'll learn how to:

✔ **Determine** when a homosexual man may be a danger to himself and others

✔ **Understand** the difference between homosexual and heterosexual activities

Why it's important:

✔ Understanding the biological reasons behind the gay man's inability to drive could help save lives.

Gay Men Can't Drive

Have you ever seen a homosexual male parallel park a car? It's a long, exhausting process! First, they circle the block looking for another spot, then reluctantly reapproach the danger zone. They'll overshoot, they'll undershoot, and they'll transition from drive to reverse with dozens of tiny adjustments. Their passenger will exit the car to assist and almost get hit. They'll FaceTime a straight male for advice. They'll either leave the car sticking out two feet from the curb or just totally abandon it in frustration.

Gay men also have issues parking in normal spaces, turning, switching lanes, and operating most machinery larger than a vape pen. Below are the chances of disaster, dependent on the machine.

GAY MEN AND MACHINES: HOW DANGEROUS ARE THEY TOGETHER?

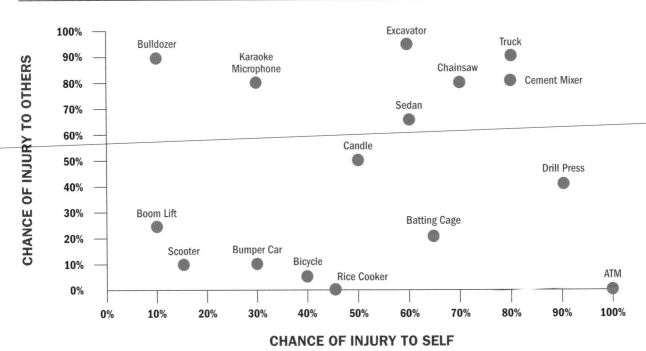

The Work of Dr. Wendy Williams

We still wouldn't understand this correlation today if it weren't for the work of **Dr. Wendy Williams**.

Dr. Williams, the keynote speaker at the National Conference for Science and Hot Topics.

A recent PhD graduate with a focus in musculoskeletal biology and celebrity shit-talking, Dr. Williams was determined to prove that gay men don't deserve to be bullied based on stereotypes. They deserve to be bullied based on facts!

She began her research on the differences between heterosexual and homosexual wrist anatomy and found something remarkable.

The Male Wrist

Most humans are born with the same hand and wrist biology, but additional parts begin to develop during male puberty.

Heterosexual men grow **heterocarpals**: additional bones that provide them with support and strength to allow them to participate in certain activities like casting fishing lines, making basketball free throws, gripping clubs, drinking out of red solo cups, turning the volume up when "Mr. Brightside" comes on, reaching for gym shorts when it's unseasonably warm outside, waving their hands in the air and calling it "dancing," or writing an email properly.

A straight man playing grass hole, an activity that uses the heterocarpals.

Homosexual men do not develop these parts, but instead acquire an entirely new ligament: the **phaggatus totalis**.

This extremely flexible ligament provides gay men the opportunity to express themselves and enhance their communication skills, giving their stories the theatrics they deserve!

With their loose wrists, homosexual men lost the ability to be good drivers. Dr. Williams found their hands couldn't sufficiently grip a steering wheel while simultaneously holding onto an iced coffee while also adjusting the volume of a hot Kylie track to the maximum level that their Nissan Leaf would allow.

STRAIGHT MALE HAND

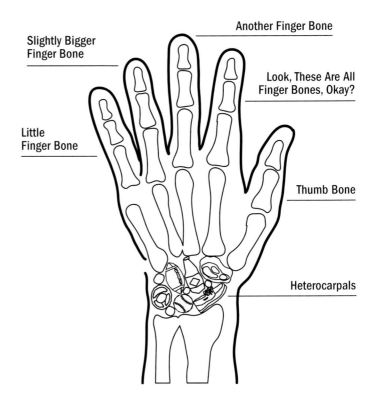

Slightly Bigger Finger Bone

Another Finger Bone

Look, These Are All Finger Bones, Okay?

Little Finger Bone

Thumb Bone

Heterocarpals

GAY MALE HAND

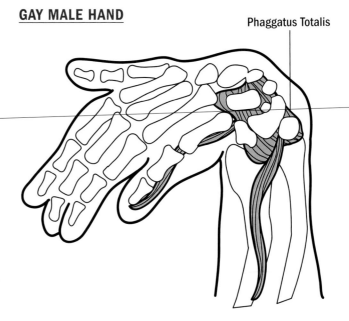

Phaggatus Totalis

One of these vehicles had a driver with extreme phaggatus totalis.

Queer Virtual Reality

All LGBTQ+ people experience the first few years of their lives as if in a simulation. As the world around them does not reflect their own internal realities, they are forced to make choices and decisions for a different, artificially constructed version of themselves. This causes a significant shift in their perceptions of time, space, velocity, and who actually wants to fuck them.

When LGBTQ+ people come out and start making authentic choices, **queer vertigo** occurs. Spatial awareness decreases as gay men lose all physical perspective. They are disoriented! They ask themselves: How far away is that curb? How wide is this car? How can the rearview mirror show what's behind me if I'm looking in front? Should I be blocking my field of vision with this dramatic hat?

To make matters worse, most gay men are unfamiliar with the physical dimensions of the vehicle they're driving because it's a rental, and their actual car is in the shop . . . from a previous accident.

A gay man telling a story like a sus velociraptor.

FAGTOID!
Most gay car accidents happen while parallel parking.

Serving Conclusions

→ **Get that jackhammer away from that gay man before he hurts himself.**

→ **That drill press isn't much better . . .**

Why Do Gay Men Color Their Hair in a Crisis?

The Tea: If his hair is bleached, approach with caution.

The Crisis Bleach

Your gay friend just dyed his hair in response to a job loss, or a breakup, or he just learned that James Corden was cast in yet another musical film adaptation. Is there no God?

Molting

Some creatures benefit by casting off certain parts of their bodies. This is known as **molting**, or exfoliating your problems.

For example, arachnids cast off their exoskeletons so they can grow. They also become reclusive and fast for long periods of time before shedding their old appearance—not unlike a homosexual man having a mental breakdown. This new appearance allows gay men to feel like a different version of themselves. It's how they run away from their problems: by leaving them unresolved in their old bodies!

TOP: A snake working to drop its bad reputation. MIDDLE: A penguin waiting for the rest of his winter trauma to fall off. BOTTOM: Kim Kardashian shedding her BBL.

Signaling

The natural world uses **signaling** as a warning to others. Gay men also do this with bright-colored hair to tell friends and acquaintances: *I'm not well right now. Please give me space.* If there's a public meltdown over the brunch menu, the hair color will work as a signal to others that a gay man is having a crisis.

TOP: The granular poison frog tries to look toxic by being all, like, red and stuff. MIDDLE: Λ mantis shows deimatic behavior by standing up straight, which apparently some animals are scared of? Lol. BOTTOM: Opossums are dramatic as hell and pretend to die when they're stressed.

A Drag Queen Explains

WELLNESS CHECKS

If you see a friend bleach or color his hair, check on him. See if he's posted any erratic stories on his social media channels, created a new profile on a niche dating site, or started posting his nudes on LinkedIn.

ONE BRUNCH SERVER TO ANOTHER:

"That man with bleached hair started crying when I told him we were out of shakshouka. He must really be going through it."

REASONS FOR A CRISIS COLOR

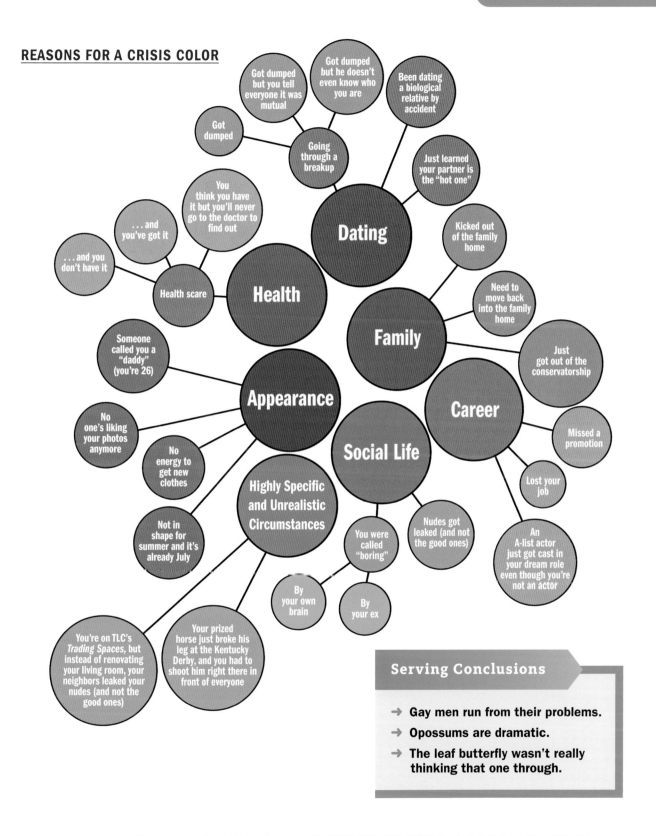

Dating
- Got dumped but you tell everyone it was mutual
- Got dumped but he doesn't even know who you are
- Been dating a biological relative by accident
- Got dumped
- Going through a breakup
- Just learned your partner is the "hot one"

Health
- You think you have it but you'll never go to the doctor to find out
- . . . and you've got it
- . . . and you don't have it
- Health scare

Family
- Kicked out of the family home
- Need to move back into the family home
- Just got out of the conservatorship

Appearance
- Someone called you a "daddy" (you're 26)
- No one's liking your photos anymore
- No energy to get new clothes
- Not in shape for summer and it's already July

Career
- Missed a promotion
- Lost your job
- An A-list actor just got cast in your dream role even though you're not an actor

Social Life
- You were called "boring"
  - By your own brain
  - By your ex
- Nudes got leaked (and not the good ones)

Highly Specific and Unrealistic Circumstances
- You're on TLC's *Trading Spaces*, but instead of renovating your living room, your neighbors leaked your nudes (and not the good ones)
- Your prized horse just broke his leg at the Kentucky Derby, and you had to shoot him right there in front of everyone

Serving Conclusions

→ Gay men run from their problems.

→ Opossums are dramatic.

→ The leaf butterfly wasn't really thinking that one through.

GAY EXPERIMENT

Using Flowers to Explain the Crisis Color

Use food dye to make a carnation's tips change color, just like a gay man's hair.

LEVEL OF DIFFICULTY: LOW | **LEVEL OF GAY:** MEDIUM | **TIME SUGGESTION:** 20 MINUTES

Materials

- Red food dye
- A white carnation
- Scissors
- A small vase

The Steps

1. Take a fresh, innocent, white carnation, and cut off a bit of the stem.
2. Pour some water into the vase.
3. How much trauma did your carnation go through? Put in a few drops of food dye for a financial issue, more for a health scare, and the entire bottle if it's a breakup.
4. Place your homosexual carnation in the vase and wait six hours.
5. Revisit your carnation, and notice that its petals are pink now, just like the hair of a homosexual who's going through it.

NOW TRY THIS!
If you add too much trauma, your carnation may not survive. See how much it takes, and report your findings!

Why Do Gay Men Love the Worst Music You've Ever Heard?

The Tea: It's all pots and pans, and not the cooking kind.

Get PrEPared

You'll learn how to:
- ✔ **Determine** what music is gay
- ✔ **Understand** what makes it gay

Why it's important:
- ✔ It's not rude, just a fact.

When a Gay Gets the Bluetooth

If your gay friend is in the passenger seat of your Uber, he's controlling the music. Here's what you might expect:

Manufactured Girl Pop
- Any British girl band
- An industry plant (ironically)
- 90's pop girl nostalgia

Showtunes
- A Broadway ballad
- "Never Enough" from *The Greatest Showman*
- "Never Enough" from *The Greatest Showman*, but it's a circuit remix

A DJ's Set on SoundCloud
- A pop mash-up they heard on Fire Island

THE GAY SOUND SPECTRUM

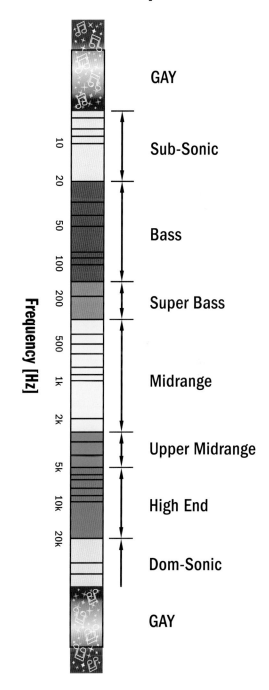

Audio Spectrum

Frequency [Hz]

	GAY
10	Sub-Sonic
20	
50	Bass
100	
200	Super Bass
500	
1k	Midrange
2k	
5k	Upper Midrange
10k	High End
20k	Dom-Sonic
	GAY

- That year's Pride Mix
- A set from Burning Man they don't remember

A Song about Fucking
- Something by Kim Petras
- Something by CupcakKe
- A song where the lyrics are "fuck me fuck me fuck me" over and over

Hyperpop
- A modem trying to connect to the Internet
- A dial tone on molly

Ironic Listens
- Something so bad it's good
- An attempt to resurrect a pop diva's flop era

Acoustics

Deep inside the inner gay ear next to the cochlea, is the **dycklea**. When triggered by gay sounds, it fills with blood and provides homosexuals with a greater auditory range, beyond the limitations of the boring heterosexual spectrum. This does a few things.

First, it allows gays to understand better subtext in conversation (which we explain more on page 157). Second, it allows them to hear the intricate nuances of a musical composition. While a song may seem "basic" to someone with rudimentary ear biology, those with advanced acoustic reception understand the complexities.

Taste

The **two-axis cultural taste chart** lets us know where music lands depending on how obscure, popular, interesting, or boring it is:

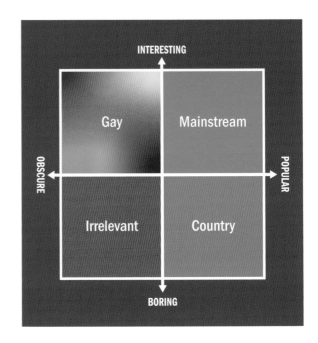

Music that falls within the **gay quadrant** has to be interesting or campy enough to grab the attention of homosexuals while staying relatively obscure. *Example: any music dropped by a Real Housewife.*

On the opposite corner of the chart, popular yet boring music lands in the country quadrant. This is a quadrant for straight male country singers only. *Examples: Luke Bryan, Jason Rhett, and Cole Brown.*

If the music is obscure enough, but totally boring, then it lives in the **irrelevant quadrant**. *Example: honestly, we don't even know what's in here because it's irrelevant.*

If something gay becomes too popular, then it hits the **mainstream quadrant**. If the people who bullied you in high school know the lyrics to a song, it's definitely not a gay thing anymore. *Example: Lizzo.*

If an artist in the mainstream quadrant falls out of relevancy with the general population, gays may readopt it as iconic and bring it back into their quadrant. *Examples: when Tove Lo went indie and Fergie's National Anthem performance.*

However, if a white female entertainer cuts her hair, she is immediately removed from the gay quadrant and placed in

gay jail until it grows back. *Examples of entertainers who've spent time here: Katy Perry, Emma Watson, Maggie Rogers, Jessie J, and Anne Hathaway.*

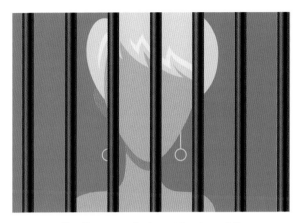

Katy Perry spent the longest time in gay jail and has been released, but is still on probation.

Did you hear the new Maggie Rogers?

Not until she grows her hair back.

What about Doja Cat?

Oh, she can do whatever she wants with bars like that!

Serving Conclusions

→ **Only gays like hyperpop.**
→ **Katy Perry should never cut her hair again.**

What Are Guncles?

The Tea: The guncle clout is real.

Get PrEPared

You'll learn how to:
- ✔ **Understand** where gay uncles came from
- ✔ **Identify** the three guncle types
- ✔ **Familiarize** yourself with the lesbiaunt

Why it's important:
- ✔ Guncles are the backbone of every family unit (if they want to be).

Why We Have Guncles

A **guncle**, or a gay uncle, is an evolutionary safety mechanism that counterbalances the high mortality rates of biological fathers. Guncles allow young children to retain a next-of-kin protector if their dad is devoured by wolves, or leaves in the middle of the night.

The Three Types of Guncles

Dedicated Guncle

This emotionally and physically available homosexual considers his nieces and nephews a blessing. You might find him proudly showing disinterested gay men a video he took of a toddler he's related to doing absolutely nothing.

The dedicated guncle hangs the kid's terrible macaroni art on his fridge next to all his same-sex wedding save-the-dates.

EVOLUTIONARY SAFETY MECHANISM

A nuclear family and their guncle.

The biological father is eaten by wolves.

The guncle replaces the biological father.

A dedicated guncle will keep stale food art forever.

Real-Talk Guncle

This guncle treats his nieces and nephews like grown adults. Open-source and unfiltered, he opts for fast-tracking and real-world advice, letting kids know that they can and should modify and customize everything in their lives.

This guncle will stage a puppet show to reenact how the **Taylor Swift and Scooter Braun drama** went down. He coaches his nieces and nephews on the best kids for them to connect with at recess for social gain. He also encourages his kin early on to consider who their chosen pop diva will be.

This is right when Scooter takes Taylor's masters.

Disappearing Guncle

Children are aliens to the disappearing guncle. He finds their mannerisms too confusing and unpredictable. Though this guncle is usually out of the loop, he may sometimes appear to have a close relationship with his nieces

A gay man moments before posting this photo to social media and ignoring this kid for another year.

and nephews because he exclusively uses them for photo opportunities to attract the attention of the dedicated guncle.

What Are Lesbiaunts?

Lesbiaunts, or lesbian aunts, were born out of a biological need to have someone cool in the family. And when it comes to gift-giving, a double-income-no-kids lesbiaunt duo is unmatched.

Serving Conclusions

→ **You really gotta love a kid to keep their art.**

→ **Teach them how Mariah Carey escaped Tommy Mottola, but with puppets.**

→ **We wish we had a lesbiaunt.**

Why Do Gay Guys Like Them Big?

The Tea: So much hole.

Get PrEPared

You'll learn how to:

✔ **Understand** the homosexual need for a large penis

✔ **Compare and contrast** homosexual holes

Why it's important:

✔ This information will prove useful when you end up in a d-hole.

Gay man thinking about big dick.

How Big Is It?

If you're a homosexual man, you probably skipped right to this chapter. You're obsessed with big dick, and you're not alone. The fascination with hung men is an inescapable part of gay culture. Gay men love big, floppy, enormous wieners because of how their anatomy is structured.

Gay man thinking about big dick.

FAGTOID!
"Hung?" is the most-common first response on gay dating apps.

Gay man thinking about big dick.

The First Hole

1–2 inches

A gay man has more than one hole, and a larger instrument can provide deeper penetration to fill them all. Most everyone reaches the **first hole**, the anus. This and the prostate can provide a nice experience for the homosexual.

The Second Hole

7–9 inches

If the instrument is big enough, it can enter the **second hole**. This is just past the rectosigmoid junction and into the sigmoid colon. This is a deeper level of satisfaction, initiating full-body chills and a single, powerful teardrop.

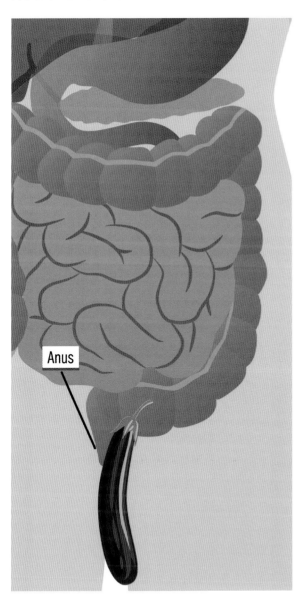

Anus

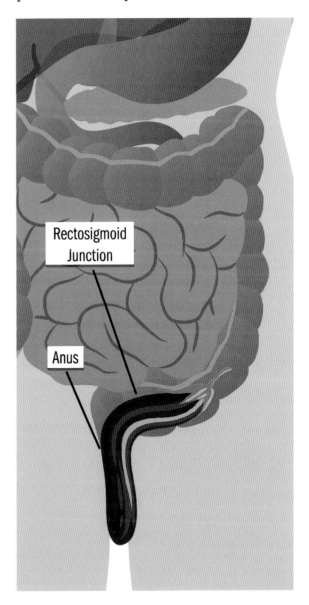

Rectosigmoid Junction

Anus

The Third Hole
10+ inches

Ultrahung men can enter the **third hole**: the large emotional void caused by homosexual trauma. The filling of this hole provides the homoscxual with feelings of affection, inclusion, self-worth, and even hope!

This hole was first discovered by **Dr. Rocco Steele**, a pioneer in third hole research, who has dedicated his life to filling the void.

Filling the third hole can also cause the gay to disassociate and end up in a **d-hole**, a highly desired deep state of bliss. It mimics the feeling therapy provides but doesn't require insurance, referrals, or a co-pay.

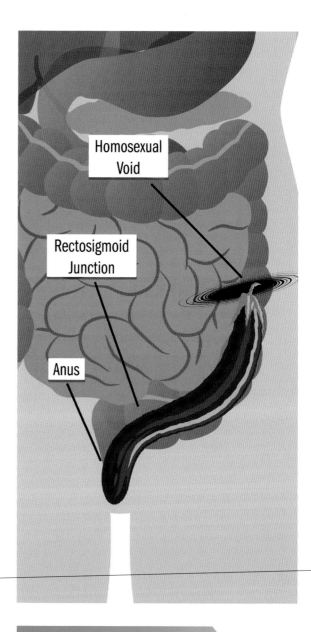

Homosexual Void

Rectosigmoid Junction

Anus

Someone in the Top 2% of OnlyFans Explains

THERAPY

Many gay men opt for a hung man over a therapist. Because therapy starts in the brain, it has to penetrate many layers of tissue to reach and fill the third hole, which can take a lifetime! A big, huge monster wiener can get there in 30 seconds.

Serving Conclusions

→ New sexy phrase: "Yes, baby, right past the rectosigmoid junction!"

→ That's all your trauma, babe.

→ Therapy is expensive.

LGBTQ+ Bacteria, Viruses, and Diseases

The Tea: Remember to wash your hands with soap! Oh, not with that one—it's decorative.

Get PrEPared

You'll learn how to:

✔ **Compare** different types of diseases that affect the LGBTQ+

✔ **Consider** how seemingly harmless things could kill a homosexual

Why it's important:

✔ Keep the community healthy.

Sickening, No?

There are some pathogens which can cause illness, death, or, in extreme cases, boredom that only affect queer people and their communities.

Bacteria

Bacteria are objects, ideas, or people that can be beneficial to the LGBTQ+ in small numbers. When they multiply, however, they can cause serious complications.

Heterosexuals in Suits (*Jos. A Bancillus*)
One straight guy in a suit can be so "daddy." He's essential for a new job, signing a lease, or filing taxes. But too many suited straights in one area will send shivers down a gay spine.

Why are there so many of them here? It's never good news. This might be the site of:

- **A straight person's wedding**
- **A business conference**
- **A formal nightclub in Las Vegas**
- **Court**
- **Church**
- **The "December to Remember Sales Event at Your Local Neighborhood Lexus Dealer"**

A Drag Queen Explains

STRAIGHT WEDDINGS

Any number of things at a straight wedding can make a queen sick, like:

· A hashtag that's a real stretch (#TaylorMadeForOneAnneOther)

· Mason jars with random shit in them

· Mustaches on sticks

· The Electric Slide

· Sweaty uncles

You can survive by befriending the one lesbian in attendance. You can spot her quietly taking her meds before the reception speeches begin.

Children (*Migrainella*)

Hanging out with a kid relative for a few hours can be pretty cool. Kids remind homosexuals of a time when they expressed themselves freely, before they had to tuck it all away to appear mysterious at gay bars. But several children? Hell. Dozens of tiny little people with wet hands who fight, scream, want attention, and climb all over the furniture. Just twenty minutes around multiple children can leave any member of the LGBTQ+ community bedridden for days.

Obligations (*Thatsenoughoccocus*)

One obligation, like watering a plant every few days, gives a homosexual some purpose. Multiple obligations will put their body into a state of shock.

A gay man silencing his notifications even though he has nothing going on.

Viruses

Viruses hit the LGBTQ+ immune system much harder and all at once. These are challenging to kill.

Conversations with Uber Drivers about the "Game" (*Sporttalkvirus*)

"Do you know the score of the game?" A phrase from an Uber driver that could make a gay heart stop. They have barely started a twenty-minute ride and are already hit with a double hate crime: a chatty Uber driver and a harrowing conversation topic. Shutting this question down may only open the gay up to other topics like politics, or worse, the driver's deteriorating marriage. Gay Science recommends that gays keep a saved note in their phone that says they're mute to show the driver.

A gay man showing his driver a note that reads "I AM MUTE" to avoid Sporttalkvirus.

A Conservative Mom with a Microphone (*Religivirus*)

If a Christian conservative white mom has a microphone and two minutes to speak, it will cause an LGBTQ+ to feel flu-like symptoms. Because they are bored and have never known good sex, colonies of religiviruses take out their frustrations on the public. You'll find them present at city council or school district meetings to discuss banning color sequences that mimic the rainbow. Though this virus is loud and uncomfortable, it's nothing an LGBTQ+ immune system can't handle.

Anything That Sounds Like It Might Be an Xbox Game (*Slurvirus*)

Watchfall, Red Warfare, Call of Madden—any word mash-up that sounds like this could cause a queer to flatline.

A religivirus demanding that the school board explain why her husband has Grindr installed on his phone.

Trigger Warning: Homophobia.

Fungi

Fungi are hard to spot at first and slowly infiltrate the system. Though they may have initial appeal, it's only a matter a time before they kill off LGBTQ+ in massive numbers.

Chris Pratt (*Prattaspora*)

A charming, funny, relatable **Chris Pratt** once made quite an impression on everyone—only to be elevated even further by his new muscle daddy status. Then things went south after he left gay icon **Anna Faris** and started posting about his church. But most unforgivable of all: He became a serious person. Homosexuals felt betrayed by this fungus. After being voted "The Worst Chris in Hollywood," it became clear that the gays were having an existential crisis and needed to protect themselves from this threat.

Disney Live-Action Remakes (*Nostalgiastoma*)

This fungus was initially embraced by the LGBTQ+ but has now led to a full-on brain rot. Wanting to support classic movies that defined their childhoods, queer people

No Melissa McCarthys were harmed in the application of this "makeup," though many drag queens were.

have been forced to sit through an assault on their nostalgia with lifeless CGI and makeup that wouldn't make it on *RuPaul's Drag Race*. We do love a Black Ariel, though.

The State of Florida (*Delusionella*)

With its nice weather and amusement parks, the state of Florida holds an iron grip on the United States. What was once a few eccentric news stories became a full-blown psych ward. A gay inferno. This is one of the most dangerous LGBTQ+ fungi because it doesn't consider reason, logic, or reality.

A GAY MAN RECOVERING FROM PRATTASPORA:

"If Chris Evans ever does a Chris Pratt, I don't think I'll ever trust a man in Hollywood ever again."

Serving Conclusions

→ Straight people love mustaches on sticks.

→ Anna Faris is a gay icon.

→ We don't hold Melissa McCarthy accountable for her Ursula makeup. She, too, is a victim in all this.

Do Lesbians Hate Electricity?

The Tea: Hollywood has some explaining to do.

Get PrEPared

You'll learn how to:
✔ **Compare and contrast** the technology in lesbian love stories
✔ **Explain** how electricity is made

Why it's important:
✔ Doing your part will help debunk lesbian myths.

Why Don't Lesbians Have Electricity in Their Movies?

In all forms of media, modern technology and lesbian love seemingly cannot coexist. Why are lesbians always caged birds in the 1800s with no air conditioning? Why are they hooking up only after churning butter?

Women in the 1800s churning butter.

Have lesbians been keeping their aversion to technology a secret from us? Why does Melissa Etheridge want us to wait by the light of the moon? Does she not own a lamp?

In this car: Two women falling in love without unlimited wireless data in *Carol* (2015).

LESBIAN LOVE IN A PIONEER HOME:

"First we make butter, Rebecca. Then, we scissor."

UNAVAILABLE TECHNOLOGY IN LESBIAN ROMANCES

	Bicycle	Telephone	Light Bulb	Penicillin	The Internet
The Bostonians (1984)				NO	NO
Carol (2015)					NO
The Favourite (2018)	NO	NO	NO	NO	NO
Colette (2018)		NO	NO	NO	NO
Dickinson (2019)				NO	NO
Gentleman Jack (2019)		NO	NO	NO	NO
Portrait of a Lady on Fire (2019)	NO	NO	NO	NO	NO
Ammonite (2020)		NO	NO	NO	NO
The World to Come (2020)		NO	NO	NO	NO

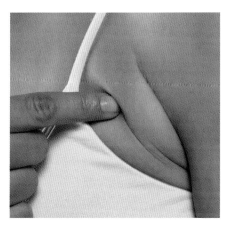

Who needs technology when you can finger an armpit in *Portrait of a Lady on Fire* (2019)?

Nothing says lesbian love like fossils in *Ammonite* (2020).

Lesbians only wear corsets and speak in innuendo in *The Favourite* (2018).

This data might lead you to believe lesbians don't use electricity, but you'd be wrong. They not only use it, they produce it!

Sapphic Electricity

At the **Tori Amos Institute of Sapphic Studies**, a randomized double-ended, double-sided study showed that queer women hold 500 percent more electricity in their bodies than heterosexuals. This is known as **lestricity**.

Sometimes electrons jump from one atom to another to another to another. But if you're about to slut-shame them, think again, Nancy Reagan! This electron shift is what causes electricity.

In lesbian atoms, these electrons just won't slow down and are all like, "Can I move in now?" This causes an even greater electrical charge. Luckily, lesbian bodies are able to handle this current.

LESBIAN VS. NONLESBIAN ATOMS

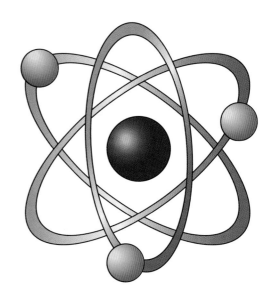

Nonlesbian Atom

A Lesbian Explains

PARANORMAL ACTIVITY

Our good listening skills and high electrical charge gives lesbians the ability to communicate on the same frequency as ghosts and other phantom entities. And sometimes I have sex with them.

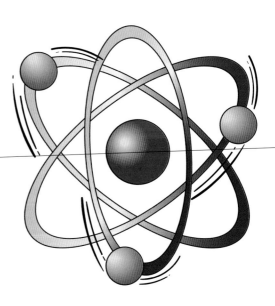

Lesbian Atom

Though lestricity is harmless to the lesbian, it can wear out their clothes quite quickly. This is why lesbians will buy ten pairs of the same exact jeans. Lestricity also gives golden retriever lesbians their wild side in the bedroom, provides gay women with a stronger connection to paranormal activity and ghosts, and inspires new technologies and thought. It's why you can find so many lesbians living in college towns where they pass their energy on to fresh students of higher learning.

A lesbian wears jeans she owns nine more pairs of.

A liberal arts college is full of lestricity.

FAGTOID!
You may spot currents running through a lesbian's body in the form of hair undercuts and sidecuts.

A FESTIVAL ATTENDEE:

"I heard Tegan and Sara are the sole power source of the Coachella Ferris Wheel each year."

The Sapphic Grid System
Sapphic electricity is an essential part of our power grid!

SEQUINS OF EVENTS

They often wear Tevas or Birkenstocks to contain the energy they produce in a closed-circuit system.

Lesbians transfer their natural currents through their carabiners to their keys.

They use their keys to enter their homes, which they share with their partner (of two weeks).

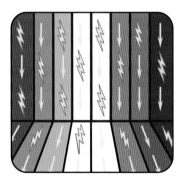

The lestricity is integrated into a complex grid system . . .

. . . that powers entire communities!

OVERHEARD IN A HEAT WAVE:

"Jane Lynch literally saved us from a power outage. I don't know what we would have done without her lestricity."

Serving Conclusions

→ Lesbians love ghosts.

→ Lesbians move in with each other quickly, and we won't make this joke anymore.

→ Actually, we will make this joke again two chapters from now.

Why Do Queer People Age Differently?

The Tea: Benjamin Button was gay.

Get PrEPared

You'll learn how to:

✔ **Understand** why some straight people look like shit

✔ **Explain** why gay people are so hot

Why it's important:

✔ It's rude to ask twin brothers why the gay one looks so much better.

Straight People Age Like Lettuce

The El-Gee-Bee-Tee-Cue-Plus look better than their cis, straight friends who are the same age. Let's break down why.

Humans age due to **free dadicals**, heteronormative molecules inside the body that react to the patriarchy and fuck you up. Increased acceptance of patriarchal influences in one's life correlates with a decline in external appearance. This takes the worst toll on heterosexual white men, who are the most unaware of the patriarchy's impact.

Two straight friends who think it's "gay" to hug. They are both 30 years old.

PATRIARCHAL STRESS

Healthy cell

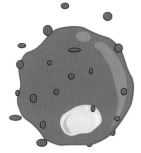
Free dadicals attaching themselves

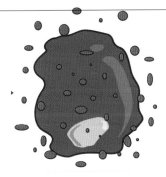
The patriarchy putting the cell through it

Siri, Play "Break Free" by Ariana Grande

Because queer people have canceled their subscriptions to a dominant part of society, they can now do whatever they want in life.

A gay after coming out.

They opt for decisions driven by their own happiness rather than conforming to set expectations. Once they've already faced disappointment from their family after coming out, they may as well choose the career they want to have, the location they want to live in, and the friends they want to be around. LGBTQ+ look younger because they are living freely.

Because heterosexuals aren't forced into this pivotal self-discovery, many believe they must endure continuous minor hardships for no reason—all in the name of tradition or what's expected of them!

They will go to a bad restaurant with people they despise and still convince themselves it was a fun time. They'll gaslight their own brains into believing that sitting through a full two-hour mass on Easter is quality family time.

Have you ever seen a queer at a country club? Absolutely not. They're not joining a club to play the same eighteen (had to look that one up) holes year after year. They're out dancing somewhere or making art from recycled yarn.

The hottest person at a country club.

Serving Conclusions

→ **No SPF can save you from the patriarchy.**

→ **My dad still won't hug me.**

Why Do Gay Relationships Feel Longer than Straight Ones?

The Tea: Five months? That's like five years on a gay timeline.

Get PrEPared

You'll learn how to:

✔ **Understand** why gay dating feels like speed dating

✔ **Compare** gay and straight dating timelines

Why it's important:

✔ Gay love is just as important as straight love, even if it only lasts four days.

Straight vs. Gay Dating

There are many differences between heterosexual and queer relationships! Ten years into dating, you'll rarely see:

- **A heterosexual couple that actually still likes each other**
- **A lesbian couple who socialize with more than six friends annually**
- **A gay couple make it that long**

Why are they on different timelines? We can only share theories because there isn't much actual science behind how we experience time. That's because time is a theoretical social construct created by humans, and more specifically, Cher.

Cher turning back time.

Let's take a look at the different relationship curves these three groups have.

RELATIONSHIP CURVES

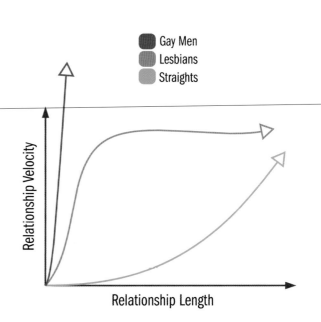

Gay Men
Lesbians
Straights

By the time straight people are on their third date, lesbians have combined and hyphenated their last names, and gay men have already broken up . . . with their next partner after the first one.

Heterochronic vs. Homochronic Timelines

There are two main reasons for the difference in how straight people and the LGBTQ+ experience the time continuum.

Actual Time

Gay men have no patience for literally anything and need you to get to the point. The homosexual experience always skips the built-in tutorial even though these gays could really use it.

Lesbians lead more accelerated lives because they grasp things faster than their straight counterparts. They can fill in the gaps. They despise small talk. They know where this is going, so they skip to the good stuff.

Perceived Time

While a straight man is only able to be on one date at a time, a gay man can be on several simultaneously.

Though it may seem like homosexuals are rushing through things, this accelerated timeline allows them to experience *more* in life than heterosexuals. Or at least that's what they keep telling themselves.

GAY MEN AT A RESTAURANT

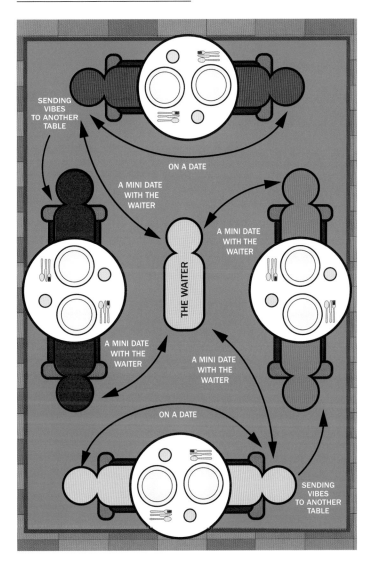

Serving Conclusions

→ **Cher invented time.**

→ **This is the last joke about lesbians moving in together quickly, we swear.**

Gay Face

The Tea: Poor thing has resting gay face.

Get PrEPared

You'll learn how to:

✔ **Understand** why a gay man's face is so goddamn gay looking

✔ **Compare** different gay faces

✔ **Explain** who the gay cousin of physics is

Why it's important:

✔ The pressures of homosexuality have a significant impact on appearances.

What Is Gay Face?

You just know when you see it. That's a homosexual face—one of the gayest I've ever seen, come to think of it.

For centuries, scientists couldn't understand what made a gay man's face look so gay. Some gay men have a blazingly fruity face, even if it's at rest and not judging ugly decor. After a few debunked theories about gay men being perpetually dehydrated from heavy amounts of socializing, one man found the answer.

THE OB DOCTOR WHEN YOU WERE BORN:

"Who needs gaydar when you have a face like that?"

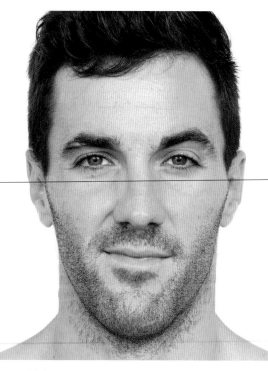 

LEFT: A man without gay face. Notice how not gay he looks? RIGHT: A man with gay face. Undeniably homosexual-looking facial features.

The Physics Behind Gay Face

Isaac Newton's gay cousin, Fig, developed the **law of gravi-slay-tion.** In addition to the downward gravity of earth's mass, gay people are subjected to other forms of gravity that affect their facial structures differently than the straights.

Fig Newton is known as the Gousin of Physics.

Inward Gravity

These are elements that pull gay men's faces inward, coming from the pressure they feel within. Some examples include:

- **The weight of their own queer existence**
- **The expectation to choose a career that Dad doesn't find to be "too gay"**
- **The pull of nonstop pop bops playing in their head**

YOUR DAD, PROBABLY:

"A theater degree?"

GAY FACE

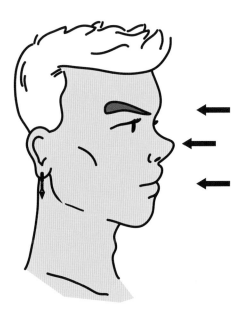

Inward Gravity

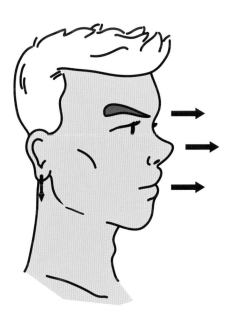

Outward Gravity

Outward Gravity

Exterior elements like people, places, and parties all pull the face outward. This pull, combined with inward gravity, result in a distinctly gay-looking face. Some of these extrinsic gravitational forces include:

- **An obsession over the personal lives of people they don't know**
- **A pull toward that new gay guy in town as they try to figure out if he's actually hot or just new here**
- **The external pressure to RSVP to a straight person's wedding even though they know something gay and fun will pop up that weekend**
- **An intense attraction to a tall man with no personality who shows no interest in you**
- **The inescapable thought that something more fun is happening elsewhere**

A gay man wondering what Dorinda Medley is up to.

Is he actually hot or just new here?

FAGTOID!

Some ethical dilemmas have both inward and outward gravity, like when a gay craves Chick-Fil-A.

Should I go to my sister's wedding next summer?

The Side Effects of Gay Face

In addition to giving gay men better skin, gay face develops new facial muscles and the ability to communicate multiple things at once. Guess what the gay faces below are trying to communicate, then check the key to see if you're right!

KEY:

TOP LEFT: Do you want to meet my partner? We're open.

TOP MIDDLE: Can I have a hit of your vape?

TOP RIGHT: You call that good music?

CENTER LEFT: I'm hating this conversation.

CENTER MIDDLE: I won't remember you in the morning.

CENTER RIGHT: Does this party have a dark room?

BOTTOM LEFT: When Beyoncé says "Everybody on mute!" you mute. What don't you understand?

BOTTOM MIDDLE: I've been stalking you for months.

BOTTOM RIGHT: Hey, it's me from before. And this is my partner. Remember, we're open.

Serving Conclusions

→ Justice for Fig Newton's erasure from heterosexual science books.

→ He's normally a 6, but he's an 8 when he moves to a new city.

→ Really though, what is Dorinda up to?

What Is Bi Panic?

The Tea: There's no button under the desk for this one.

The Bisexual Mind

Does the bi mind become overstimulated when surrounded by multiple genders? Oh, absolutely. Let's dig into the physics and bi-ology behind this specific and intense phenomenon, (and why they all wear Doc Martens).

Bi Gravity

While **monosexuals** are subjected to the standard laws of gravity, bi and pan people exist with a gravitational pull in multiple directions. It's sort of like being the most desired person at the party, but the other way around. This chaotic force causes bi-sensory overload and destabilization of the bisexual individual.

BI GRAVITY

Monosexuals

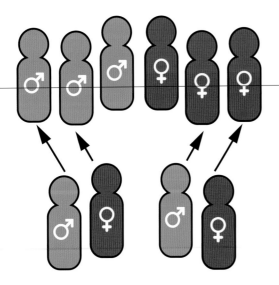

Bisexuals and Pansexuals

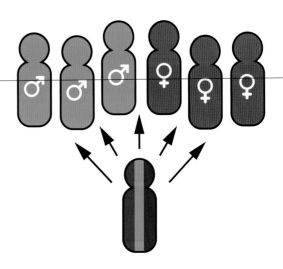

Bi-Panic Scenarios

Some common scenarios when bi panic sets in:

- **Standing in a room and thinking, "Why is everyone here so goddamn hot?"**
- **Finding an attraction to different-gender siblings and fantasizing about them**
- **Knowing it would be easier to date a woman, but unfortunately falling in love with a man**

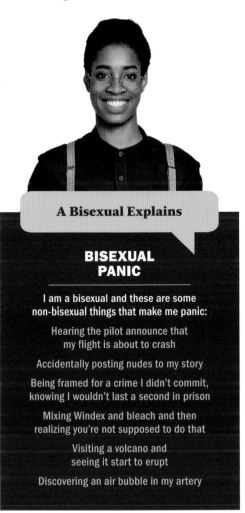

A Bisexual Explains

BISEXUAL PANIC

I am a bisexual and these are some non-bisexual things that make me panic:

Hearing the pilot announce that my flight is about to crash

Accidentally posting nudes to my story

Being framed for a crime I didn't commit, knowing I wouldn't last a second in prison

Mixing Windex and bleach and then realizing you're not supposed to do that

Visiting a volcano and seeing it start to erupt

Discovering an air bubble in my artery

Bi-Stabilization

Though this type of panic can be an unsettling gravitational experience, bisexuals have found a few different solutions.

Balance

This is why bisexuals sometimes wear horn-rimmed glasses, which act as a balance beam for the head.

Grounding

Others opt for septum piercings, so the magnetic force can pull them to the earth's core and center them more easily.

Cooling

Grounding may initiate heat buildup in the ankles, which is why you may see a bi person cuffing their pants. They may also use rubber to offset the heat induction, most commonly with Doc Martens.

Serving Conclusions

➜ **Bisexual health scares got *Buffy* canceled.**

➜ **Septum piercings do more than just look cool.**

Fluid States Of Matter

The Tea: Let's find out how loose your sexual molecules are.

Get PrEPared

You'll learn how to:

✔ **Understand** how sexual fluidity works just like other forms of matter

Why it's important:

✔ Different people are all different kinds of horny, and that's okay.

This won't end well.

Where Do We Keep Our Sexuality?

Everything in the world is matter, but not everything matters in the world. That paper court summons you received is made of matter, but it doesn't matter if you show up because no one runs your life but you! (Also, don't take legal advice from a *Gay Science* textbook.)

Though that summons is a solid, some properties of matter can take on different forms depending on how much energy is added or subtracted.

For example, ice (solid) can turn into water (liquid), which can turn into water vapor (gas). And the solid food you're eating at this highway rest stop could turn to gas later if your digestive system isn't having it. And possibly even liquid if it's a *really* bad day.

But what does this have to do with who we're attracted to?

Like all other matter, sexuality is comprised of sexual molecules in the body that are loosely or tightly packed. This determines who we're attracted to. While some molecules remain unchanged, molecules of sexually fluid people change between different states of matter.

FAGTOID!

Another type of matter, *Family Matters*, ran for nine seasons!

STATES OF SEXUALITY

Increasing Arousal

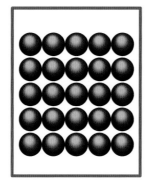 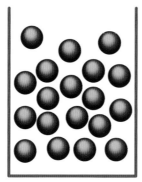 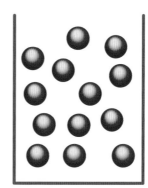 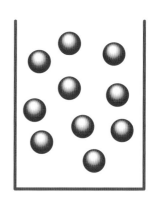

Homosexuality/
Heterosexuality

Homoflexible/
Heteroflexible

Bisexuality/
Pansexuality

Horny

Homosexuality/Heterosexuality
These tightly packed molecules hold firm in their attraction to the same or opposite gender.

Homoflexible/Heteroflexible
These are relaxed molecules that mostly stick with the same or opposite gender, but not always! A **heteroflexible** guy might touch a dick. A **homoflexible** girl might let a guy watch her ride his girlfriend.

Bisexuality/Pansexuality
These loosely packed molecules allow bisexual and pansexual people to find attraction across several different genders.

Horny
Horny people have the loosest molecules, so they're willing to do anyone, anywhere, anytime. Completely feral and utterly insatiable, they'll flip between multiple dating apps while in a meeting at the office, then get off in the private breastfeeding room. Not that we know anything about that.

Serving Conclusions

→ **Don't eat at Roy Rogers.**
→ **You're probably at least a little gay, be honest.**

The Gravitational Pull of Gray Sweatpants

The Tea: It's VPL time.

Sweats Szn

When cooler weather hits, **gray sweatpants** seem to attract the attention of gay men in the area. They are mesmerized by this casual, comfortable, and otherwise unremarkable piece of apparel when other men wear it. Locking eyes on the garment, they'll thoughtfully inspect it (right in the center) for any rips, tears, or manufacturing issues. Then they'll look up at the man wearing it and see him in an entirely new light.

This phenomenon has yet to be solved by modern science, though many theories exist that attempt to explain why gay men are so fixated on joggers. First, let's understand the subject better.

A Gray Ally

Are gray sweatpants part of the LGBTQ+ Awning? Sort of! They belong to a special class of allies that mark a safe gay space. These allies provide mental, emotional, or spiritual assistance in times of stress, anxiety, isolation, or danger. They don't ask questions. They don't judge. They give you the help you're seeking.

There are widely accepted theories that help explain the attraction.

Unremarkable gray sweatpants.

Magnetic Pull Theory

Queer magnetic pulls are not an uncommon occurrence. Lesbians are profoundly drawn toward female-heavy historical reenactments and zookeeper uniforms. Bisexual women? Gamer boys with ADHD.

The most popular theory is that there is a magnetic pull occurring between the sweatpants and the homosexual's eyeballs. If you rub a bit of iron against a magnet, it will cause a magnetic field to form. It's the rubbing between the gray sweatpants and the long iron underneath it that attracts the pole-seeking homosexual.

Black Hole Theory

Some scientists have deviated from the magnet theory and propose that there's something much greater at work here: a black hole. Gray sweatpants gravity (also known as **grayvity**) is so strong that no amount of gay attention can escape it, and may even approach the event horizon: the boundary surrounding the sweatpants beyond which nothing can escape.

If the pull is hung enough, a gay may be sucked into the wearer's sweatpants forever, like when Carol Anne is sucked into the TV in *Poltergeist*, or when Chris falls into the sunken place in *Get Out*.

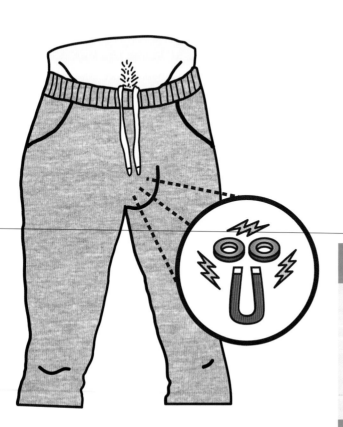

FAGTOID!

Gay men have disappeared in the Bermuda Triangle after a hung ship captain chose to wear gray sweatpants at sea.

Serving Conclusions

→ If you didn't attract magnetism while wearing gray sweatpants, that's okay. Some people are born with other gifts instead.

→ Gray sweatpants have absolutely nothing to do with your penis.

The Periodic Table of LGBTQ+ Elements

1 Ta Taste																	**2 D** Disco
3 W Wig	**4 Mh** Mesh																**5 Aw** Award Shows
6 C Camp	**7 Bl** Hair Dye	**8 Wx** Witchcraft													**9 Tm** Trauma	**10 A*** Ast*r*isk Shaming
11 Sp Speed	**12 Ct** Cutoffs	**13 Dy** DIY	**14 F** Fiber	**15 Su** Brunch											**16 Ax** Anxiety	**17 Sv** Survival Movies
18 Th Theatrics	**19 P** Piercings	**20 A** Artisan Goods	**21 Se** Club Soda	**22 Dp** Nudes											**23 La** Late	**24 Wi** Wet Wipes
25 Cd Candles	**26 Co** Cottages	**27 Ff** Fan Fiction	**5678 Ch** Choreo	**28 Fa** Mom's Favorite	**29 E** Eyeliner	**30 G** Paranormal	**31 Bk** Blockers	**32 B** Binders	**33 Ov** Overreacting	**34 V** Vibrato
35 S Succulents	**36 H** Hands	**37 U** Undercuts	**38 Pr** Purebred Rescues	**39 Cb** Cold Brew	**40 Cu** Cuffed Clothes	**41 Dh** Dropping Hints	**42 X** Molting	**43 T** HRT	**44 Ds** Dysphoria	**45 Ht** Hot Topic
46 L Lighting	**47 Cr** Carabiners	**48 St** Staying In	**49 Go** Going Out	**50 O** Open Relationships	**51 Pi** Panic	**52 Dr** Boots	**53 Do** Double Puberty	**54 J** Joy	**55 He** Fissures	**56 Po** Amyl Nitrite

57 Bf Ride-or-Die From HS	**58 Rx** Local Pharmacist	**59 Fe** Playable Female Character	**60 Sm** Stage Managers	**61 Cw** Coworkers Who Gossip	**62 En** English Teacher	**63 Q** Quiet Car

64 Ga Gaga	**65 Br** Britney	**66 Ch** Cher	**67 Ju** Judy	**68 M** Mariah	**69 Ja** Janet	**70 Ba** Barbra	**71 K** Kylie	**72 Md** Madonna	**9/4 By** Beyoncé	**9–5 Dp** Dolly

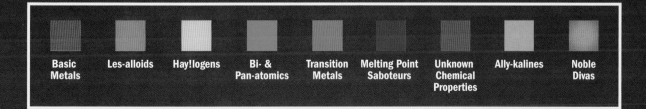

Basic Metals   Les-alloids   Hay!logens   Bi- & Pan-atomics   Transition Metals   Melting Point Saboteurs   Unknown Chemical Properties   Ally-kalines   Noble Divas

Basic Metals

These are basic elements that can be found throughout queer culture. They are the essential LGBTQ+ foundations and include things worn on the body like wigs and mesh. Queer people have good taste sometimes, but also enjoy bad taste (in the form of camp).

Les-alloids

Elements like witchcraft and fan fiction mainly affect lesbians, but are also bi-coded.

Hay!logens

These gay male elements are usually found in large groups and are extremely reactive to one another.

Bi and Pan-atomics

Bisexual and pansexual people associate with elements like cuffed jeans and sleeves. Another core element: dropping hints that they're not straight, though they aren't afraid to tell you explicitly.

Transition Metals

Trans people are very familiar with these metals and share the unique experience of having a second puberty. Except this time, it's more expensive!

Melting Point Saboteurs

These are personal demons that try to derail queer success and happiness. LGBTQ+ people deal with at least one every day.

Unknown Chemical Properties

These are elements that are not technically queer but feel like they are. These gay-jacent chemical components can be found on the Internet when you see one person shaming another by r*m*v*ng the vowels, and in any location where someone is making use of their vibrato.

Ally-kalines

These elements are core allies who support LGBTQ+ people in different stages throughout their lives. That butch girl in all black who stage-managed every one of your high school productions? She wasn't gay, but she had your back! And God bless other allies including playable female characters like Sonya Blade in *Mortal Kombat*, your local pharmacist, and an empty seat on the quiet car on a train ride home.

Noble Divas

These are the 11 core pop divas that provide the most iconic bops for the LGBTQ+ community. Every 10 years they meet to induct a new diva, though they often just end up absorbing her powers.

AT THE MEETING OF THE DIVAS:

"Ashley Tisdale? Oh, we absorbed her."

GAY EXPERIMENT

Elements Experiments

It's time to become a proper gay chemist and start doing some chemical experimentation! See which new fruity outcomes will occur when you combine two or more LGBTQ+ elements.

LEVEL OF DIFFICULTY: LOW TO HIGH | **LEVEL OF GAY:** MEDIUM TO HIGH | **TIME SUGGESTION:** ???

Materials

- Every element on the periodic table

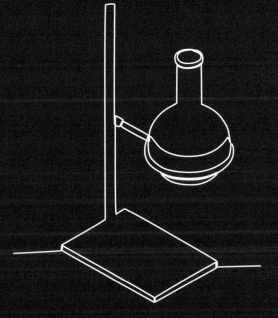

The Steps

1. Learn about the potential outcomes when combining elements. There can be (1) a formation of a new or existing compound, (2) a positive or negative chemical reaction, or (3) instant death.
2. Try combining elements! Here are some of our favorites:

DIY + Hair Dye = Panic

Vibrato + Quiet Car = Violent Chemical Reaction

Staying In + Going Out = The Entire LGBTQ+ Umbrella

Amyl Nitrite + Fissures = Local Pharmacist

Nudes + Hands = Staying In

Amyl Nitrate + Mom's Favorite = Panic + Anxiety

Theatrics + Open Relationships + Coworkers Who Gossip = Ast*r*sk Shaming

Theatrics + Witchcraft = Paranormal + Open Relationship

DIY + Local Pharmacist = Instant Death

Why Do Women and Gay Men Get Along So Well?

The Tea: A timeless bond. Literally iconic.

Get PrEPared

You'll learn how to:

- ✔ **Identify** different types of queer chemical bonds
- ✔ **Differentiate** between what the gay best friend trope has told us and what real science proves
- ✔ **Understand** the history of the girls and the gays

Why it's important:

- ✔ Historical perspective is essential to understanding this unbreakable bond.

Queer Chemical Bonds

The salt on your food, the caffeine in your cold brew, and the alcohol you drink alone every night are all chemical bonds! These bonds are everywhere. The very air you're breathing right now has oxygen in it, which is probably a chemical compound but definitely a thing that trees poop out into the atmosphere. You're breathing in tree poop. But enough of that! We're here to explore queer chemical bonds.

These unbreakable bonds occur between at least one element of the LGBTQ+ and something outside of it. Before we explore the iconic bond between the girls and the gays, let's take a look at some other LGBTQ+ chemical bonds that are inseparable.

LGBTQ+ CHEMICAL BONDS

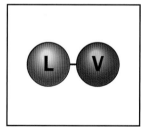

Lesbians + Vancouver

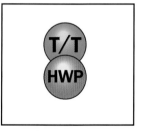

They/Them + High-Waisted Pants

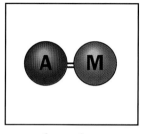

Asexuals + Meaningful Relationships

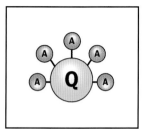

Queer + Acronyms

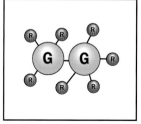

Open Gay Couples + Arbitrary Relationship Rules

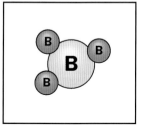

Bisexuals + Calling Random Things Bisexual Culture

Are Gays Just Handbags?

If your only exposure to gay people has been poorly written characters in American films and television shows, you might think that all gay men are just an accessory to straight women.

Gay Best Friend Tropes in Media

Here are some examples of popular GBFs from film and television:

Note: *We could not secure the rights to use reference images, so we pulled the closest stock photos we could.*
They are so close you wouldn't even be able to tell the difference, but we thought we'd let you know.

A still from the film *Clueless* (1995) where Cher Horowitz (Alicia Silverstone) uses her new sexless gay best friend, Christian Stovitz (Justin Walker), to help her snag a boy she likes.

Andy (Anne Hathaway) navigates the world of Miranda Priestly (Meryl Streep) with the help of the fashion gay Nigel (Stanley Tucci) in *The Devil Wears Prada* (2006).

In *My Best Friend's Wedding* (1997), Jules (Julia Roberts) has her GBF George (Rupert Everett) drop literally everything to make another man jealous.

Sarah Jessica Parker, Cynthia Nixon, Kristin Davis, and Kim Cattrall in their iconic roles with the witty GBF Stanford Blatch (Willie Garson) in *Sex and the City* (1998).

Are straight women out there collecting gays like Pokémon then discarding them as soon as a hot straight guy comes around? What about lesbians? Do they even mix well with the gays? These tropes are outliers that overshadow a long-standing beneficial relationship between the two groups.

Mutualism

Our natural world is full of mutually beneficial ecological interactions. Crocodiles and birds have an especially interesting kink. Occasionally, after a meal, a crocodile will open its jaws and a plover bird will just fly right inside! A major power-bottom move, as the bird will eat the food out of the crocodile's mouth and fly away unharmed. One gets a meal and the other gets a dental cleaning.

A professor of gay bestie studies at the **Chromatica Institute** found a unique chemical connection between the gay man and the straight female that mimics mutualism. These bonds create an ecological relationship that has a net benefit for three primary survival needs: shelter, protection, and nutrition.

Shelter
Roommates

A girl and a gay talking shit about their third roommate while she's out with her boyfriend.

Protection
Walking together in public

A girl and a gay walking home from the bars at 2 a.m. after talking shit about their former third roommate.

Nutrition
Keeping each other fed

A girl and a gay grabbing wine before they talk shit about their new third roommate.

Gay-onic Bond

The **gay-onic bond** occurs between *gay men* and *queer women*. It's a hyperstrong electrostatic attraction between oppositely charged homosexuals. Their differences pull them together, like a queer magnet.

Gay men provide good company for queer women who want to enjoy a friendship with a man without any unwelcome advances. In return, queer women keep gay men grounded. Thirsty gays can really gas each other up to increase their chances of a hookup. This is why so many of them surround themselves with the company of other gay men!

Queer women do no such thing. They keep it real. If you're familiar with a gay man who doesn't have a lesbian in his life, he probably needs a reality check. But don't tell him this. Get a lesbian to do it.

Actual conversation between two gay men:

The same conversation between a gay man and a queer woman:

Delete that story!

GAY-ONIC BOND

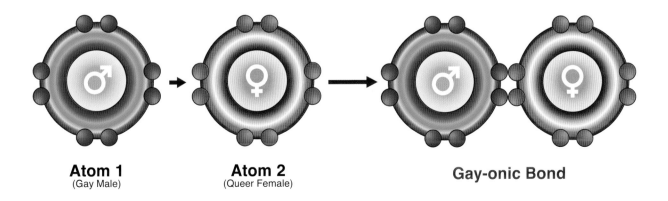

Atom 1
(Gay Male)

Atom 2
(Queer Female)

Gay-onic Bond

Gay-valent Bond

The **gay-valent bond** occurs between *gay men* and *straight women*. They share an electron that makes them both attracted to and disappointed by men.

Gay men will give straight women valuable feedback on their relationships with men and help call out red flags. In return, gays get to see the dick pics.

Gay Men and Straight Women Commonalities

- Going out of their way to return a shopping cart

- Doing poppers on the dance floor

- A passion for organized fitness

- Getting the Gardasil shot

- Taylor Swift

- Bravo shows

Actual conversation between a gay man and a straight woman:

Tomorrow let's take a prison bootcamp workout class

The one where they make you check your clothes at the front like it's jail?

Yes! Benny B. is doing an Eras Tour themed one

I'm going to lose it at the Illicit Affairs remix

What about after?

I have a date later

Is it with big 🍆 Chad?

That's right I showed you his pic

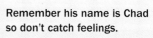

Remember his name is Chad so don't catch feelings.

GAY-VALENT BOND

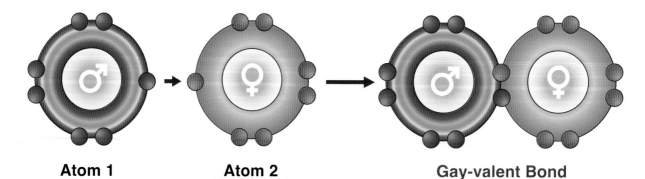

Atom 1
(Gay Male)

Atom 2
(Straight Female)

Gay-valent Bond

GAY-ONIC AND GAY-VALENT BONDS THROUGHOUT HISTORY

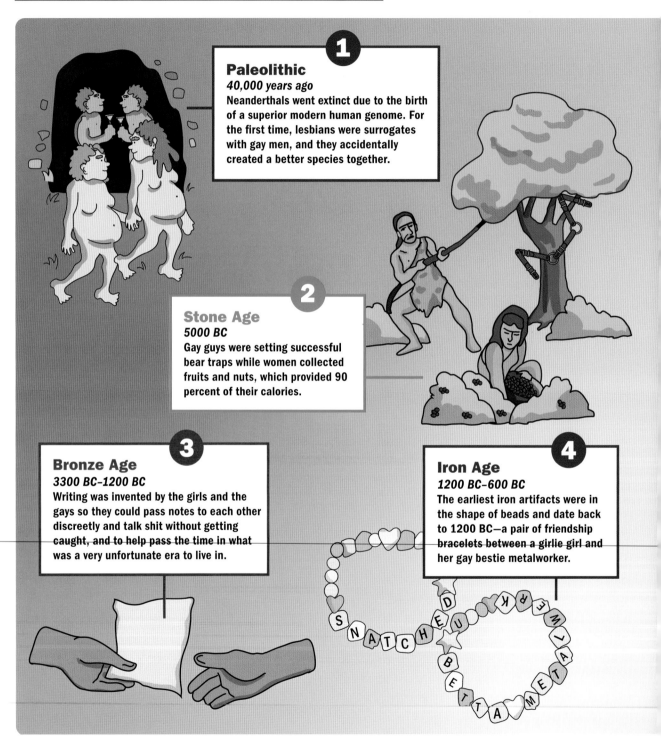

1

Paleolithic
40,000 years ago
Neanderthals went extinct due to the birth of a superior modern human genome. For the first time, lesbians were surrogates with gay men, and they accidentally created a better species together.

2

Stone Age
5000 BC
Gay guys were setting successful bear traps while women collected fruits and nuts, which provided 90 percent of their calories.

3

Bronze Age
3300 BC–1200 BC
Writing was invented by the girls and the gays so they could pass notes to each other discreetly and talk shit without getting caught, and to help pass the time in what was a very unfortunate era to live in.

4

Iron Age
1200 BC–600 BC
The earliest iron artifacts were in the shape of beads and date back to 1200 BC—a pair of friendship bracelets between a girlie girl and her gay bestie metalworker.

5 Classical Era
400–800 AD
A mercantile class rose up in the first half of 7th century AD, mainly led by ambitious merchants made of childless gay men and power lesbians.

6 The Middle Ages
1200 AD
The printing press was codeveloped by gay men and lesbians. Gays were looking for a way to automate their work while lesbians wanted to find a solution to preserve the condition of their hands.

7 The Renaissance
1450 AD
Sick of Gregorian chants, the girls and the gays introduced secular music because they really needed something they could dance to.

8 Age of Revolution
1800 AD
The American Revolution occurred after the girls and the gays abandoned their Greenfit tea diets and dumped the rest into Boston Harbor.

Other Examples of Modern Bonds

Since the turn of the 21st century, scientists have seen all sorts of new bonds form between the girls and the gays.

The School Bond

Girls enjoy being around a boy they can actually trust, and the gays need the girls to simply survive public school.

If a boy is sitting with all girls at a lunch table, he's definitely gay.

The Professional Bond

Corporate besties who overanalyze their coworkers and send each other gay memes all day.

Liz is on the work chat discussing this season of *Yellowjackets* with her work gay.

The Mother-Son Bond

This bond is why a mom has more energy when she's around her son.

A mom staying up past 8 p.m. because her son is visiting.

The Teacher-Student Bond

English teachers and their gay students have a certain understanding.

A gay student and his English teacher discussing his classmate Laura's recent pregnancy scare.

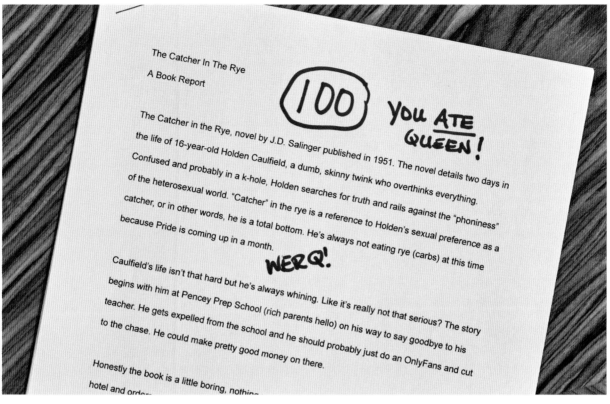

The Catcher In The Rye
A Book Report

(100) YOU ATE QUEEN!

The Catcher in the Rye, novel by J.D. Salinger published in 1951. The novel details two days in the life of 16-year-old Holden Caulfield, a dumb, skinny twink who overthinks everything. Confused and probably in a k-hole, Holden searches for truth and rails against the "phoniness" of the heterosexual world. "Catcher" in the rye is a reference to Holden's sexual preference as a catcher, or in other words, he is a total bottom. He's always not eating rye (carbs) at this time because Pride is coming up in a month.

WERQ!

Caulfield's life isn't that hard but he's always whining. Like it's really not that serious? The story begins with him at Pencey Prep School (rich parents hello) on his way to say goodbye to his teacher. He gets expelled from the school and he should probably just do an OnlyFans and cut to the chase. He could make pretty good money on there.

Honestly the book is a little boring, nothing hotel and order

A gay boy's paper on *The Catcher and the Rye*, graded by his teacher.

The Therapist-Patient Bond
A woman is a better listener than any man, and a therapist who has a gay patient is guaranteed income forever.

"So I cried for two minutes and then posted it to my story."

The Gay Man and Iconic Actress Bond
This is a bond between gay men and the older actresses who they talk, text, and post about constantly as if they know them personally. This is a one-sided bond.

Serving Conclusions

→ Lesbians keep it real.
→ There is absolutely no difference between the stock images we used and the real stills, and you wouldn't have known the difference if we didn't tell you.
→ Moms will murder for their gay sons.

How Does Gaydar Work?

The Tea: How are we gonna find our people in this dangerously heterosexual environment?

Get PrEPared

You'll learn how to:

✔ **Understand** how gaydar is triggered

✔ **Assess** the benefits and risks of gaydar

✔ **Differentiate** the magnitudes of several gaydar events

Why it's important:

✔ Understanding your gaydar is the first step to unplanned sex in public.

What is Gaydar?

Gaydar is a superior genetic trait specific to gay people that allows them to identify one another discreetly. It evolved out of necessity to survive the bizarre world that heterosapiens have created with things like religion, cryptocurrency, and eating fondue at the mall.

The Melting Pot inside a mall: straight culture.

Homotremors

Sharing a similar geological effect as earthquakes, queer people send and receive **homotremors** through the ground. These are small vibrations that only they can feel, which oscillate at the same frequency as Mariah's whistle tone. This is why a Taylor Swift concert induces record-breaking seismic activity and how the subterranean worm monsters found Reba McEntire's queer-coded energy in the movie *Tremors*.

The *Tremors* worm sensing that Reba McEntire's character probably eats pussy.

Here are some of the more common ways these gay earthquakes are triggered:

Gay Whiplash

Gay whiplash occurs when two gays make a first pass at eye contact, followed by a second, faster, double take. This subtle reaction reverberates into the ground and activates gaydar. These signals are so strong that two men could be wearing oversized Polo shirts and Margaritaville boat shoes at a Tom Clancy book signing in Memphis and still know the other is gay.

Lesbian Apparel Pheromones

Lesbian apparel pheromones are a special type of vibration that travel through the air. There are some garments that just look different to gay women when another gay woman wears it. This is why some clothes and accessories like hoodies, glasses, hats, or pants look quite common on a straight woman but scream dyke on a lesbian.

Some apparel that isn't so obvious may need a secondary confirming factor, like short nails, to trigger gaydar.

A GAY WOMAN PICKING UP ON LESBIAN APPAREL PHEROMONES:

"The way she's wearing that sweater vest? That's a dyke right there."

A woman wearing a beanie.

The same beanie sending lesbian apparel pheromones.

Thirst Traps

A photo of a straight man without a shirt on? The camera just caught him like that. A photo of a gay man without a shirt on? He *specifically wanted* a photo like that. This is how gaydar is triggered when a photo of a shirtless man is posted on social media.

You'll know which one's gay because he'll be standing alone with a lack of purpose and a palpable desperation to let other gays know *he has a body*. This desperation is familiar to every gay man and he'll feel the digital homotremors.

Male vs. Female Gaydar

While homotremors are violently obvious to queer men, women prefer to send and receive smaller, subtler quakes. Further complicated by their high electrical charge, bisexual and gay women will sometimes miss these signals and mistake them for friendliness. The desire for another woman to be gay will also shroud their receiver, convincing them that any vibration is a queer one. That's just the construction across the street, babe.

When Gaydar Becomes Deadly

The cities of Sodom and Gomorrah were thriving homosexual utopias full of wine, sex, and MDMA. Located on the Jordan Rift Valley, the cities' inhabitants confused an actual earthquake for homotremors. As they congregated to initiate a citywide orgy, they were decimated by the effects of the surprising quake.

Gays excited for an orgy, but instead, they're gonna die.

A gay man forcing his less-hot friend to take this photo in front of a dumpster because the lighting was good.

How to Measure Gaydar

Gay Science quantifies gaydar quakes on the **Dichter and Chickter scale**.

A magnitude 1 quake may feel like light bass while anything over 5 is an unmistakable gay earthquake. To better understand these measurements, examine the chart below:

THE DICHTER AND CHICKTER SCALE

Magnitude	Cause
0–1	They're wearing a thumb ring.
1–2	She sits closer to women.
2–3	He follows Trixie Mattel.
3–4	They listen to hyperpop.
4–5	She's at this lesbian bar right now.
5–6	He's wearing a jockstrap but has never played a sport.
6–7	He gave him his number after the Countess Luann cabaret show.
7–8	She just ate her girlfriend out.
8–9	He ordered a vodka soda.

FAGTOID!

In an experiment at the Brenda Meeks Seminary, gay and straight men scored the same when asked to identify homosexuals from photos alone. However, gay participants did spot the other gay participants, and later, they all fucked each other.

Serving Conclusions

→ **Mariah's whistle tone will scramble gaydar accuracy, but everyone there's probably gay anyway.**

→ **What is it about the beanie?**

→ **A double take is, like, so gay.**

→ **If you're going to die in a natural disaster, it might as well be during an orgy.**

Navigating Gay Friend Groups

The Tea: Some gays are worth a long visit, while others are better for a day trip.

Get PrEPared

You'll learn how to:

✔ **Compare and contrast** the different types of gay social groups

✔ **Identify** warm and cool homosexual currents

Why it's important:

✔ Knowing how to access friend groups will help you avoid subpar friendships.

Making Gay Friends

While straight friendships come together organically for a gay person, making gay friends isn't as easy. How long should you wait before jumping into a new group? What are the dynamics within the group? What are the rules around hooking up?

Since this can be all sorts of confusing, the gay community has resorted to using sea science to help them make sense of it all.

Because being gay makes it more difficult, you'll have to identify who is being friendly and who is just horny. Can you dodge advances while also staying in their good graces so they don't retaliate against you? If women have been dealing with men like this for years, you surely can!

I'M GAY. WHY IS THIS STRANGER BEING FRIENDLY TOWARD ME?

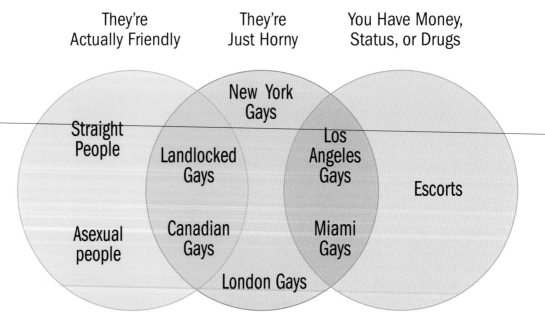

They're Actually Friendly   They're Just Horny   You Have Money, Status, or Drugs

Straight People

New York Gays

Landlocked Gays

Los Angeles Gays

Escorts

Asexual people

Canadian Gays

Miami Gays

London Gays

The Land

Gay friend groups are land masses resting upon **tech-house-tonic plates** that exist alone (as islands) or have joined up next to another land mass. These neighboring masses are associated and sometimes, but not always, intermix. When these plates move, the groups will separate and end their associations with each other.

It's common for gay friend groups to sink entirely! This happens when a group loses its goodwill or becomes irrelevant. Here are some inactive or disbanded gay friend groups of the past:

Group	Year of Sinking	Reason
Laser Tag Gays	2000–2007	Aged out
The Stacie Oricco Queens	2004	Lack of bops
The Scrapbookers	2005	Merged with Activity Gays
The WB Gays	2006	When it became The CW they migrated to the HBO gays
The Hot and Nice Ones	2015	They were actually just hot and mean all along
Prank Gays	2016	Euthanized for being annoying
Game of Thrones Gays	2019	That finale

Ocean Currents

Gay friend group navigation can be achieved by studying the patterns of ocean currents and how the temperatures of those currents affect how things flow. Step on the conveyor belt of homosexual socialization and let the ocean guide you!

Thermohaline Sis-culation

The method of entering and exiting a gay friend group is determined by a system of warm and cool currents.

Warm currents are traits and behaviors of the group that are attractive or inviting.

Cool currents are reasons to leave the group and will push you away from them and back out into the open ocean. You can learn more about these on the next page.

Wind-Driven Sis-culation

Certain major events may cause someone to move between different gay groups. In some cases, it's the only way to approach an island.

THE GAY OCEAN

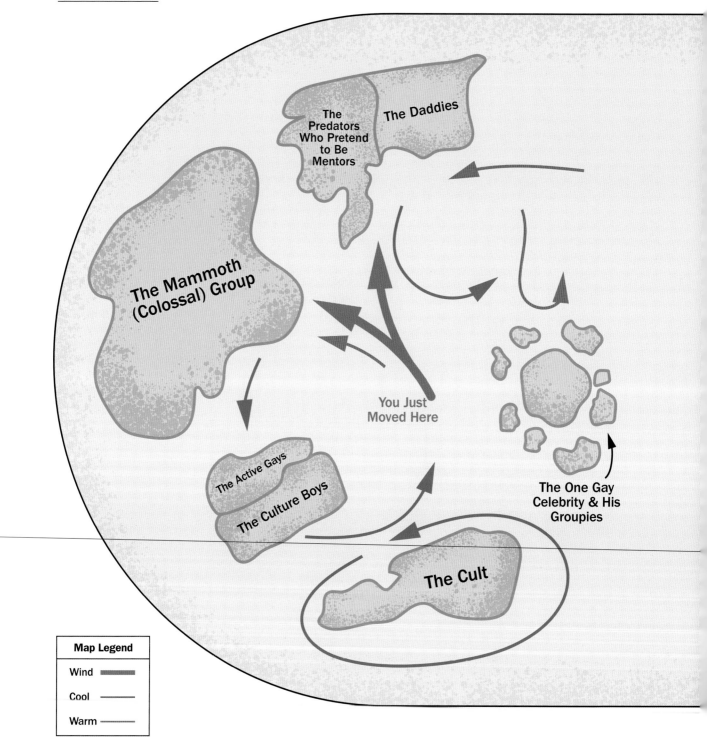

The Predators Who Pretend to Be Mentors

The Daddies

The Mammoth (Colossal) Group

The Active Gays

The Culture Boys

You Just Moved Here

The One Gay Celebrity & His Groupies

The Cult

Map Legend	
Wind	
Cool	
Warm	

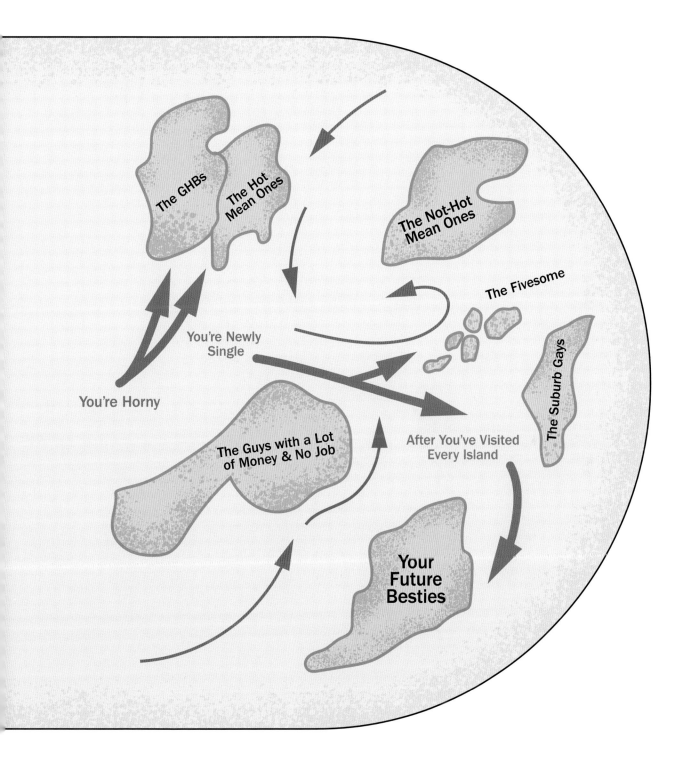

The Mammoth (Colossal) Group

- A group of 35-50 people who all somehow know one another and travel together

Warm Current: Always an invite to everything they do

Cold Current: Bothered by the one annoying gay who keeps getting away with inviting himself

The Activity Gays

- Believe that simply existing and having conversation isn't a concept
- Make matching t-shirts before the concert
- Schedule a house dinner every night at 7 p.m. on vacation
- Gamify all social activities
- Ask: How can we make this into a performance?
- Nominate one main activity gay (the camp counselor) who leads and plans everything

Warm Current: They aren't boring

Cold Current: Exhaustion

The Cult

- Eerily devoted to one another
- Party in their group, travel in their group, and never seen with new people
- Can't make personal choices without consulting the rest
- Never look like they're having fun
- Bar you from entering the cult, but permit you to look at it from afar

[no warm currents visit this land mass]

The One Gay Celebrity and His Groupies

- He was a gay on that show once and they're clinging onto that clout

Warm Current: You're such a fan!

Cold Current: You're not that much of a fan, actually

The Daddies

- Relaxed
- Confident
- Friendly
- Have money
- Over 35

Warm Current: Good conversation

Cold Current: They go to bed at 10 p.m.

The Suburb Gays

- Always free to hang
- Fine for now
- Don't work out

Warm Current: You lost your job and had to move back in with your parents for a bit

Cold Current: You moved to the city

The Hot Mean Ones

- Hot
- So mean
- Will never fuck you
- The type of mean that makes you feel invisible

Warm Current: One made eye contact with you

Cold Current: He was actually looking at someone behind you

The Not-Hot Mean Ones

- Not hot
- Mean
- You'd never fuck them
- Judge the party they're at, but don't leave
- Even meaner than the hot mean ones because they hate themselves too

Warm Current: Accidentally got pushed in their direction

Cold Current: Spending three minutes in their presence

The Predators Who Pretend to Be Mentors

- Over 50
- Assault you when you're overserved

Warm Current: You confuse them for the daddies

Cold Current: The unsettling look in their eyes when they've had a few

The Fivesome

- Two couples and a fifth wheel

Warm Current: You're invited to everything because they need a sixth

Cold Current: Realizing you'll have to date the fifth wheel if you want to continue being in the group

The Culture Boys

- See Broadway shows
- See movies while they are still in the theater
- Know award show trivia
- Watch every HBO limited series
- Know when new music is coming out

Warm Current: A desire for quick-witted banter and conversations beyond sex and drugs

Cold Current: Weren't paying attention to pop culture for a few days and now you're out of the loop

The GHBs

- They talk about DJs like they're Beyoncé
- Horny immediately
- Fall out at least once a year

Warm Current: They're fun

Cold Current: You miss having hydrated skin and a steady stream of serotonin

The Guys with a Lot of Money and No Jobs

- Travel all the time
- Work none of the time

Warm Current: Going overseas sounds fun

Cold Current: You have no money and a job

Your Future Besties

- The greatest people you'll ever meet

Serving Conclusions

→ Large gay friend groups can never effectively weed out the annoying one.

→ Activity gays work well with sobriety.

→ Not-hot mean gays will tell you the hurtful "hard truth" about yourself because they're "honest" like that.

→ You'll eventually find your besties. You just have to meet all the other groups first.

Why Are Gay Coworkers Either Best Friends or Mortal Enemies?

The Tea: Is the other office gay trying to kill you? Yes. Yes, he is.

Work Gays

In the workplace, homosexual employees have a special relationship with one another. Sometimes they are work besties, but other times they're out for blood. Work gays exhibit different behaviors with one another depending on genetic factors and the overall homosexual presence in the workforce. We use **workplace gaynotypes** to predict how any pair of work gays will interact with one another.

What Are Gaynotypes?

Have you ever wondered why some people have blue eyes and others have brown eyes? And why the people with blue eyes won't stop reminding you of that? Well, both the trait of eye color and the characteristic of being annoying were passed down from their parents, through genetics!

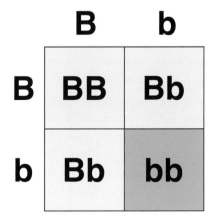

With these genes, there is a 25 percent chance the offspring will have the curse of annoying blue eyes (but a 100 percent chance we won't be friends with them).

When two gay men are placed in a professional setting, we can apply science in a similar way to predict how they might react to each other. First, let's help you understand a bit more about gay chromosomes and how dominant or submissive they can be.

INCREDIBLE BLESSING OR WORST NIGHTMARE:

"Did you hear? They hired another gay guy. Now you're not the only one."

Zygaysity is the degree to which both copies of a gay chromosome or gene have the same workplace genetic sequence. Each homosexual has a pair of alleles, a dominant trait (G) and a submissive trait (g). Their degree of similarity with another homosexual defines their relationship. A pair of alleles can be homo-heterozygous, homo-homozygous, or homo-nullizygous.

	G	g
G	**GG**	**Gg**
g	**Gg**	**gg**

Homo-heterozygous relationships (Gg) occur when the dominant and recessive trait combine in **symbioSIS**. This leads to a gay work bestie 50 percent of the time.

	G	g
G	**GG**	**Gg**
g	**Gg**	**gg**

Signs of this relationship include:

Discussing which coworkers might be gay.

Agreeing that all their coworkers are at least a little bit gay.

Sharing drug contacts.

97

Homo-homozygous relationships (GG or gg) occur when two of the same dominant or recessive traits pair up. This leads to a gay work nemesis, with either a sub or dom subtype, 50 percent of the time.

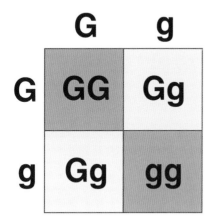

Sub homo-homozygous relationships (gg) are passive-aggressive and have a 25 percent chance of occurring.

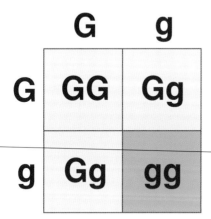

Signs of this relationship include:
- Having a condescending attitude because one thinks he's the younger, hotter one

- Having a condescending attitude because one thinks the other one thinks he's the younger, hotter one
- Microwaving popcorn all day because one knows if the other is on a low-carb diet
- Reserving the good conference room when he knows you need it

Dom homo-homozygous relationships (GG) are hyperaggressive and have a 25 percent chance of occurring.

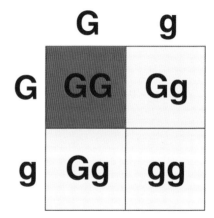

Signs of this relationship include:
- Demagnetizing the other gay guy's key card when he steps away from his desk
- Never using first names, but instead calling the gay nemesis "the other gay guy"
- Tapping gay circles to dig up the worst rumors about the other, and then breaking gay code by telling all their fellow coworkers
- Leaving threatening notes in blood

A threatening message seen in a dom homo-homozygous work relationship.

Homo-nullizygous relationships are null gay relationships that do not follow typical zygaysity rules. These occur less than one percent of the time when there is an imbalance in workplace homosexuality.

	NULL	NULL
NULL	NULL	NULL
NULL	NULL	NULL

Low homosexuality occurs when there are literally no other gays that work there, resulting in a single, unmatched allele. These are examples of professions where gays are an endangered work species:
- A construction worker (male)
- Auto mechanic
- Crypto trader
- The clergy

High homosexuality occurs when there are too many gays that work there, resulting in an equal work atmosphere. These are examples of professions with large homosexual representation:
- Flight attendant
- High fashion retail sales associate
- Hairdresser
- Ironically, also the clergy

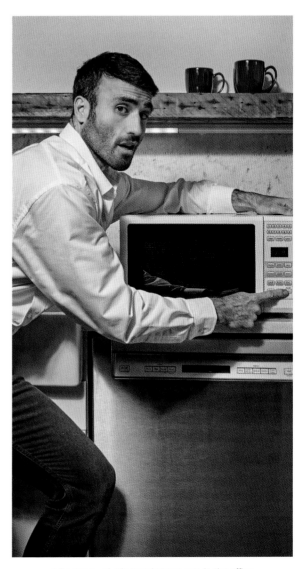

A homosexual microwaving popcorn in the office because his gay nemesis is on a low-carb diet.

Serving Conclusions

→ **Gay men can make you feel amazing.**

→ **Gay men can ruin you.**

→ **Stop telling us about your blue eyes.**

Why Do Gay Men Like Iced Coffee?

The Tea: A gay man with frostbite will still order an iced coffee.

Get PrEPared

You'll learn how to:

✔ **Understand** why hot drinks are a gay no-no

Why it's important:

✔ It's not a preference, it's a biological need.

A homosexual looking for a cold brew.

Ice, Ice, Baby

A gay man will walk into a coffee shop wearing an expedition parka during the worst winter on record and order his coffee iced. Through snowstorms and frostbite, that queen will sip his cold brew like it's 92 degrees Fahrenheit in Zipolite.

A lack of iced coffee may drive a gay man into a psychosis, which is why so many gay Americans experience culture shock when they visit Europe for the first time. An iced Americano just isn't the same, you know.

Their preference for a cold brew extends beyond enjoying things that demand additional steps. They actually fulfill significant nutritional needs! Iced coffee and cold brew satisfy two biological desires within a gay man.

Two gays going to get an iced coffee.

A gay waiting for his iced chai.

Temperature

Homosexual men run warmer than straight men. This is due to carrying the emotional stress of all their friends' real-life drama, knowing the details of their workplace drama, and keeping track of the fictional drama of at least a dozen reality shows.

An overheated gay keeping track of everyone's feuds.

Caffeine

Caffeine allows gay men to walk faster. Because gay men are, on average, late as fuck to things, walking faster allows them to be ten minutes late instead of fifteen. It also provides a rush of endorphins that only gay people can achieve by passing slower straight people on the sidewalk.

While caffeine may give others palpitations, gay people wake up with palpitations every morning by simply knowing it's a new day, and caffeine is needed for them to reach an equilibrium.

Caffeine also dilates the pupils so the eyes can absorb more light. While straight people may have a sensitivity to bright light, gay men find pleasure in shiny things. They are drawn to things like sequins, or their bag of lost drugs on the club floor glistening in the light of their concerned friend's iPhone flashlight.

THE GAY WALK

A gay litmus test being performed on hot and iced coffee.

A gay man who lost their bag of ketamine. (It's in their friend's pocket.)

FAGTOID!

If your gaydar isn't working, check what they're drinking.

Serving Conclusions

→ **An iced Americano just ain't it.**

→ **Heart palpitations are queer-coded.**

→ **Your friend had your "lost" drugs all along, but you won't find out until the next morning.**

Plant Gays, Explained

The Tea: Who needs a benzo when you have plants?

Gateway Hobby

Queer men often find themselves involved in hobbies that take very little effort to start but have the potential to go deep. An innocuous decision has now become a full investment. This is a **gateway hobby**, and having many plants is one of them. This is why many queer men will buy a succulent on a whim and end up living in the house from *Jumanji* with sixteen varieties of ficus.

A GOOD GAY FRIEND:

"Can we swing by 9th Ave? I'm plant-sitting while Dean is in Palm Springs."

Fluctuating Desires

Queer men want to feel necessary while managing the least number of obligations. Plants make gays feel like something else depends on them, but they can still take loads in Palm Springs this weekend.

These men possess a contradicting blend of an intense desire to be included and a severe indifference. Plant ownership is perfect for this. It feels like starting a group chat then muting everyone. It's still a group of friends, but with none of the noise!

A plant gay in his apartment in Silver Lake.

Conversation Bridging

Because taste in music and entertainment vary greatly between straight and queer men, every queer person holds on to at least one queer-straight topic to use in the company of straights. Talking about plants is a safe topic to mention, as well as these other options to consider:

QUEER-STRAIGHT TOPICS

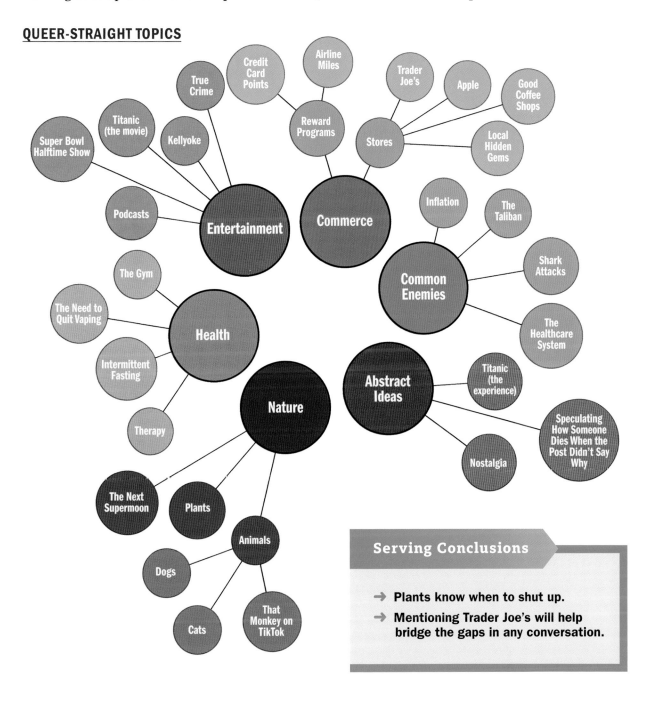

Serving Conclusions

→ Plants know when to shut up.

→ Mentioning Trader Joe's will help bridge the gaps in any conversation.

Why Can't Queer Men Remember Each Other's Names?

The Tea: You can't remember his name but it's probably the same as yours.

Get PrEPared

You'll learn how to:

✔ **Blame** your bad memory on a new disease
✔ **Manage** your anxieties

Why it's important:

✔ You should be less stressed about remembering people's names.

What's Your Name Again?

The scene: a gay party. The crime: someone couldn't remember someone else's name. But who is the perp and who is the victim? It usually sounds something like this:.

As he vents to another friend, he's reminded that he couldn't remember the other guy's name either. In fact, he doesn't even know the name of the friend he's venting to. This is a genetic disorder called namenesia and it exists primarily in queer populations. There are a few reasons for namenesia:

Hyperfocus

Queer men are often so focused on the impression they're making that they block out new information. This includes the stress of:

- **Appearing confident but approachable**
- **Getting your own name right**
- **Wondering if you've met them before and if you should have said, "Nice to see you again" instead of "Nice to meet you"**
- **. . . but now you've missed their name entirely and you've been talking for two minutes so it's too late to backtrack**

> He's so arrogant, he can never remember my name!

> Who?

> You know . . . him. That guy over there . . .

He has no fucking idea what that guy's name is.

Encoding

A queer male may not be able to remember a name because there's a lot of competition between other names and faces in their memory, especially since all the guys they've met recently seem to have the same haircut.

Half of these men are named Matt, probably.

Distraction

Queer men are easily distracted, especially when surrounded by other homosexuals.

CYCLE OF QUEER DISTRACTION

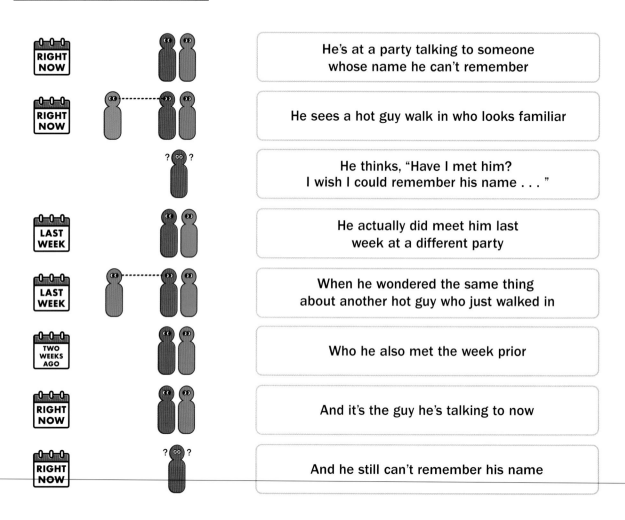

RIGHT NOW	He's at a party talking to someone whose name he can't remember
RIGHT NOW	He sees a hot guy walk in who looks familiar
	He thinks, "Have I met him? I wish I could remember his name . . . "
LAST WEEK	He actually did meet him last week at a different party
LAST WEEK	When he wondered the same thing about another hot guy who just walked in
TWO WEEKS AGO	Who he also met the week prior
RIGHT NOW	And it's the guy he's talking to now
RIGHT NOW	And he still can't remember his name

A GAY TACTIC TO REMEMBER A NAME:

"Take my phone and add your Instagram?"

Serving Conclusions

→ It's not a character flaw. It's a genetic disorder!

→ His name is probably Matt.

Why Do Gay Men Run Like That?

The Tea: Why is that run, like, super faggy?

Get PrEPared

You'll learn how to:

✔ **Identify** the parts to the gay run
✔ **Understand** how gay men have survived in the wild

Why it's important:

✔ The gay run is a superior biological trait.

Gays on the Go

The **gay run** is a restrained jog with a low center of gravity and a little bit of drama. Why do homosexuals look like they are being chased by the Blair Witch in a library? What is the biological reason for gay men running like they have to catch a train and just got a BBL?

The gay run has two major evolutionary advantages:

Deception

The gay run deceives predators. Gay men have survived for ages by employing a theatrical run that's surprisingly quick. By confusing predators into believing they're easy prey based on their body language, they're actually deceptively fast and capable of getting away. Gays *really* know when to book it.

The gay run is how Elton John got away from Eminem after their 2001 Grammy Award performance!

Nonverbal Communication

The gay run is a form of nonverbal communication used to avoid scaring off any potential female besties. The run says: "Though I am running full speed toward you, there's no need to be alarmed. I am a homosexual and this is a safe space." This doesn't mean the female bestie is entirely safe from danger, though. There's probably a good reason why the gay is running, so she better grab her shit and start running too.

THE GAY RUN

The brain is hyperaware of how gay they look when running. This anxiety gives the homosexual added adrenaline to outrun predators.

The relaxed, flicked wrist is classic biological trickery, fooling foes into thinking this will be an easy hunt.

The elbows flail like the homosexual is drowning in water. This reduces wind resistance.

The homosexual may lock their knees in place as they run, which prevents injury.

Though the rest of the body is moving dramatically, the gay's feet barely leave the ground. This helps them conserve energy.

FAGTOID!
The gay punch does not hold the same power as the gay run.

Serving Conclusions

→ **Gays are fast.**
→ **Flailing is all about wind resistance, duh.**

Gay Hookup-to-Friends Life Cycle

The Tea: Gays just wanna do it.

Get PrEPared

You'll learn how to:

✔ **Navigate** the transition from a hookup to a friendship

✔ **Distinguish** between the different stages of gay friendship

Why it's important:

✔ He doesn't hate you, it's just a cocoon stage. (Unless he hates you.)

A Gay Metamorphosis

What makes an awkward, chunky caterpillar turn into a beautiful, svelte butterfly? We literally have no idea. Now let's talk about gay stuff!

In the heterosexual world, former flings rarely become friends. But with homosexuals, it seems like every friend has a sexual history. What is different about the gays?

Because the community is smaller, interacting with a former fuck buddy is unavoidable. From the first blow job to a forever bestie, homosexuals go through a transition known as the **hookup-to-friends metamorphosis**.

LIFE CYCLE

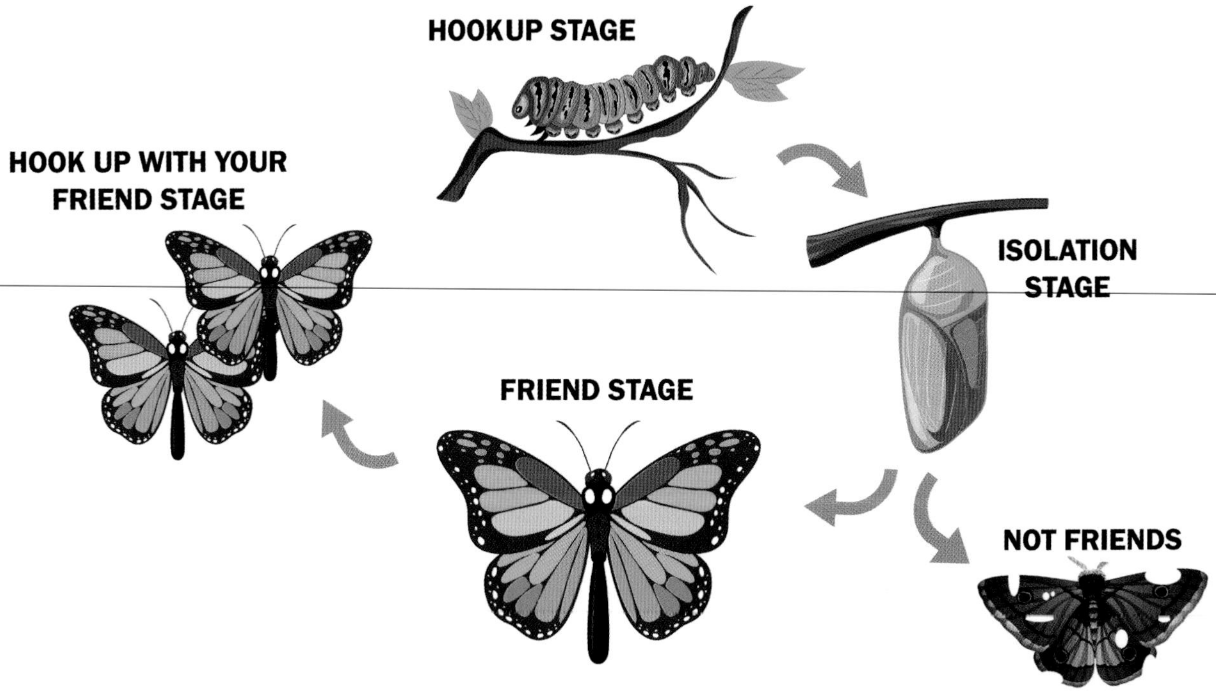

HOOKUP STAGE

HOOK UP WITH YOUR FRIEND STAGE

ISOLATION STAGE

FRIEND STAGE

NOT FRIENDS

Hookup Stage

This is the earliest stage for gay men who find each other attractive and need to do it immediately. This may be in the form of a no-talking quickie, a few hot sessions, or dating that extends into weeks.

Isolation Stage

When one or more homosexuals find diminishing returns, the hookup stage will end. This might be sudden (ghosting) or drawn out (uninterested one-word texts). It might even be because one was open but not that open. Regardless of whether either of them still feel a sexual connection, isolating (or cocooning) is necessary to protect their pride and preserve their self-esteem.

Friend Stage

Whether it's one month or a few years later, the universe has brought both homosexuals back together. Rid of their desires to seem attractive to each other, they openly discuss the most disgusting parts of themselves. The vulnerability initiates friend bonding, and they evolve into something much more beautiful than before.

Hook Up with Your Friend Stage

Sometimes, but not always, one crazy night of drugs and alcohol brings these gay butterflies back to the starting point where they may hook up once or more. Sometimes it's wild and hot, while other times it feels a bit bizarre.

Not Friends

Not every friendship can go from a hookup to a butterfly. Sometimes you end up with a moth! There are a few reasons why this can happen:

- **One of you didn't fully cocoon during the isolation stage and kept poking your head out to try to keep hooking up even though you were past that stage.**
- **One of you didn't actually cocoon and just kept hooking up with everyone's friends on the down low.**
- **One of you isn't butterfly material. (It's them, okay?)**

THE BUTTERFLY TEA:

"And a butterfly hooking up with a caterpillar? That's just weird."

Serving Conclusions

→ The gay community is small.

→ Everyone that you know has hooked up.

→ We still don't know how a caterpillar turns into a butterfly.

Closeted Hibernation

The Tea: Bears have quite the influence on gay culture.

Closeted Hibernation

Being "in the closet" isn't just an expression, it's a fact! All LGBTQ+ people live inside literal closets until they are ready to come out. The closet isn't a bad thing, it's a safe space for queer people to understand who they are. Plus, all their clothes and shoes are right there.

LGBTQ+ people may spend decades in the closet, and over time may experience **metabolic queer depression**. This phenomenon represses queerness but can never eliminate it. There are a few reasons why the LGBTQ+ stay living in a closet:

- **Preservation.** In moments and spaces where gay joy wouldn't be fully utilized, the LGBTQ+ can preserve their queerness until the time is right for them.
- **Desolation.** There aren't enough LGBTQ+ in their population, so it may be pointless to come out.
- **Safety.** They live in Saudi Arabia, Somalia, or the panhandle of Florida.

Leaving the Closet

When finished hibernating, a person may decide to announce their hibernation completion with an in-depth YouTube video or 10-part TikTok series, while others may do so quietly.

Going Back in the Closet

Some LGBTQ+ people decide to return to the closet temporarily. There are a few reasons why this may happen:

- **It's too exhausting to be gay right now.**
- **It's too expensive to be gay right now.**
- **They had to move back in with their parents.**
- **They're doing prison time.**

A queer man going back in the closet after seeing the cost of a Pride party.

Bears (Animal) vs. Bears (Gay)

What's the difference between a hibernating bear (animal), and a hibernating bear (gay)?

A BEAR (ANIMAL) HIBERNATING IN A TREE

- Has fur
- Safe from winter elements
- Loses 30% of its body weight
- Does not eat or drink
- Significant drop in heart rate
- Awake but not really
- Not horny
- Takes 2-3 weeks to adjust to post-hibernation life

A BEAR (GAY) HIBERNATING IN A CLOSET

- Has fur
- Safe from strict Sharia Law
- Gains 30% of its body weight
- Does not get tested
- Significant drop in confidence
- Alive but not really
- Very horny
- Takes 2-3 years to adjust to post-hibernation life

A HIBERNATING QUEER:

"I'm just taking a little nap in the closet so strict Sharia law doesn't kill me."

Serving Conclusions

→ It's okay to go back in the closet (especially if you're going to prison).

→ It's, like, super expensive to be gay.

Why Can't Queers Sit in a Chair Properly?

The Tea: Queers don't wanna do it your way.

Get PrEPared

You'll learn how to:
- ✔ **Understand** why queer people approach things differently
- ✔ **Identify** new uses for a church

Why it's important:
- ✔ Problem-solving and creative thinking are queer traits.

Biological Deviation

Queer people are born into a world that's not meant for them—a world created for and by straight people, where LGBTQ+ people are meant to feel like outsiders.

Heterosexual propaganda.

The natural queer approach is to do things differently.

How straights wipe vs. how gays wipe.

Functional Diversity

A heterosexual brain sees something for what it is, while a LGBTQ+ brain sees something for what it could be, and more specifically, what social event it could turn into. Conditioned to find alternative solutions, queers often discover many functions for one thing. In the following example, we see what straight people consider a church to be best used for, compared to how queer people might see it.

How straight people see a church:

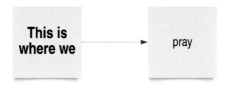

How queer people see a church:

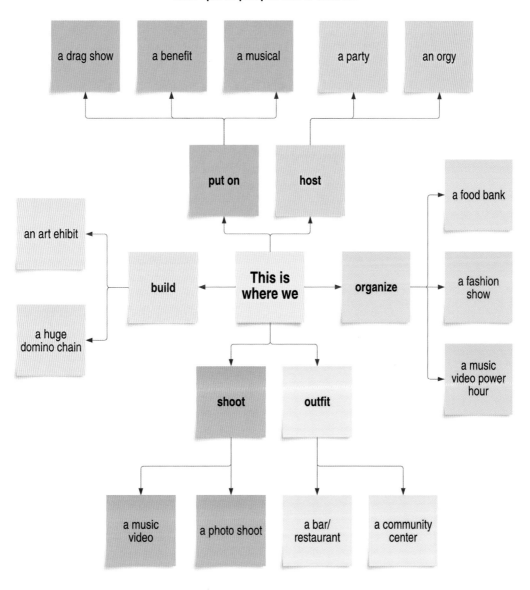

Functional diversity is also the reason why queer people:

- **Don't see the visible light spectrum as "white" but instead as many different color choices.**

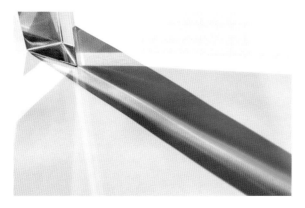

- **Renovate, paint, and upfit their apartments, even though they're just rentals.**

- **Can always get into a party regardless of the circumstance.**

They aren't letting anyone else in.

Is there someone inside that we know?

Is there an open window we can climb in through?

Have we offered them coke?

Try messaging someone on the apps who is in there.

Maybe we need to thin our group out?

We'll get someone inside and then he'll open a window.

No really have we even tried offering them coke?

Serving Conclusions

→ A queer will find a way to party here.

→ A queer will get into this party no matter what.

→ You literally can't stop a queer from getting into a party.

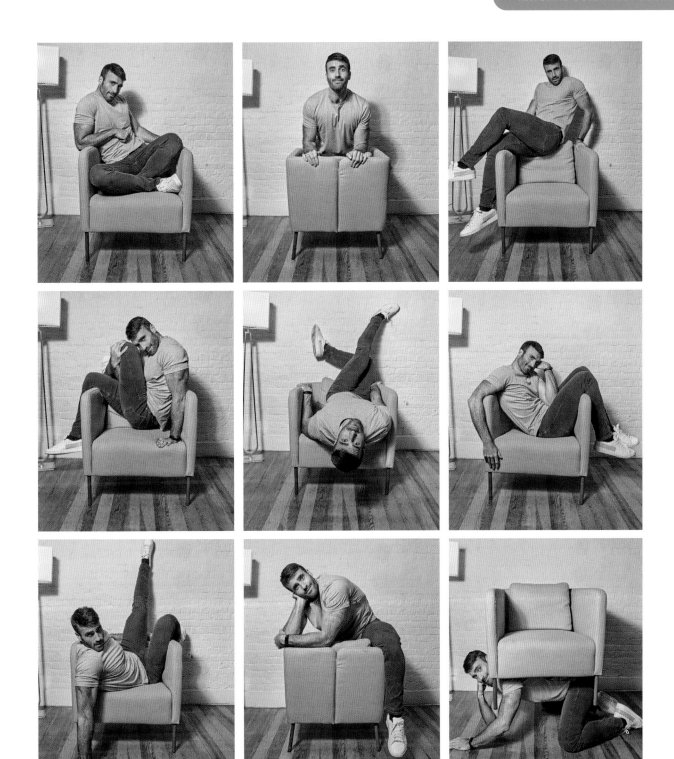

A gay man sitting in a chair.

Why Do Queer Men Love Camp but Hate Camping?

The Tea: Camp? Yes. Camping? No.

Get PrEPared

You'll learn how to:

✔ **Understand** the difference between camp and camping

✔ **Identify** the five major bi-omes

✔ **Compare** different levels of camp

Why it's important:

✔ Confusing the two could end your relationship with a queer person.

Camp or Camping?

Are we rewatching *Showgirls* or sleeping on the ground without air conditioning? Are the vibes Elton John or John Muir? Is this a **Krystle Carrington** catfight on *Dynasty*, or will we have to poop in the woods? The difference between camp and camping is obvious for most queer men. While they do favor deliberately exaggerated theatrics, there is a sliding scale to how much outdoor living they'll tolerate.

A DYNASTY ENTHUSIAST:

"Krystle Carrington never went camping. Though she was in a coma."

The Bi-osphere

American climatologist **Dr. Greta Garbo** discovered that the LGBTQ+ socialize in different terrains and habitats. She separated these into five major bi-omes.

Dr. Greta Garbo, an ecological bi-oneer.

Five Major Bi-omes

Aquatic: Queer spaces in and around water. *Example: pool party.*

Grassland: Low-density queer spaces. Here you'll find pockets of homosexuals in a calmer space. *Example: Runyon Canyon.*

Forest: High-density queer spaces. Here you'll find a lot of homosexuals, usually a safety hazard if there were ever an emergency. *Example: Pride parade.*

Tundra: Polarizing queer spaces. The spaces are not always favored by the entire community. *Example: circuit party.*

Desert: Gay dead zoncs. These are not queer spaces. *Example: Indy 500.*

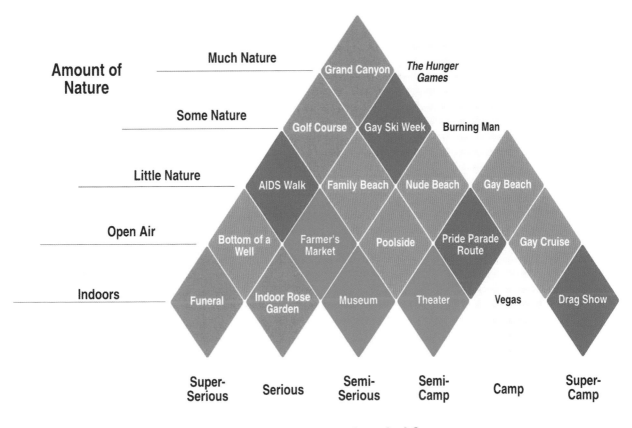

Amount of Nature

Much Nature

Some Nature

Little Nature

Open Air

Indoors

Grand Canyon · *The Hunger Games*

Golf Course · Gay Ski Week · Burning Man

AIDS Walk · Family Beach · Nude Beach · Gay Beach

Bottom of a Well · Farmer's Market · Poolside · Pride Parade Route · Gay Cruise

Funeral · Indoor Rose Garden · Museum · Theater · Vegas · Drag Show

Super-Serious · Serious · Semi-Serious · Semi-Camp · Camp · Super-Camp

Level of Camp

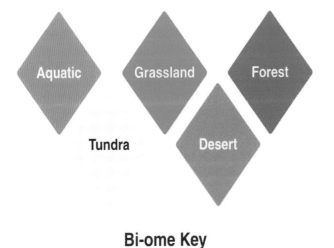

Aquatic

Grassland · Forest

Tundra · Desert

Bi-ome Key

Serving Conclusions

→ A forest bi-ome is certain death in an emergency.

→ No gay should be at the Indy 500.

→ *The Hunger Games* was both camping and camp.

Are There Signs of Queer Life in Outer Space?

The Tea: Close encounters of the queer kind.

Get PrEPared

You'll learn how to:

✔ **Understand** what is needed to sustain queer life

✔ **Identify** queerness in the galaxy

Why it's important:

✔ Knowing you're not alone can reduce anxiety. But sometimes it can cause it too. Sorry we weren't more helpful here!

Space: The Final Lacefrontier

Much of what we know about queer extraterrestrial life now was once kept a secret. Our knowledge of queer UFOs and communications with other beings was contained to **Area 54**: part air force base, part drug-fueled disco club. Because it was mostly run by white gay men, it was super exclusive. Only people with the highest security clearance and/or bubble butts could access it.

After a leak made by a queer witch whistleblower at the **Pentagram-agon**, the public became aware of the government's secret communications with fruity beings in outer space, and how incredibly queer our universe really is.

Beam Me Up, Liza!

In an attempt to contact LGBTQ+ aliens through interstellar gay-dio in 1985, scientists developed a nonbinary system of Liza Minnelli gifs that could be easily understood by any beings using non-Earth languages. The first message sent said: "Are we alone?"

Eight minutes later, Earth received a communication from the universe: "Top or bottom?"

Queer life did exist! Over the next few decades we learned that queer humans and queer aliens had a lot in common. LGBTQ+ aliens also cut their own hair in the bathroom. They think they are Matilda. They earn their humor through trauma. They live inside a bubble. They power through an insufferable TV show just to watch how the queer subplot unfolds. Finally, the LGBTQ+ weren't alone.

One Giant Leap for They-/Themkind

English physiSISt **Stephen Hawqueen** discovered that to sustain queer life an environment had to provide three basic essentials:

1. **A source of energy**
2. **Water in a liquid state**
3. **Antidepressants**

But beyond just life, Hawqueen noticed that almost every element in interplanetary and intergalactic space wasn't straight. In fact, heterosexuality is specific to Earth and has yet to be found anywhere else in our universe. Here's everything in space that's been proven to exhibit queer traits and characteristics:

The Sun
Shines brighter than any other planet in our solar system. It gives us life, hunny! It thinks everything revolves around it. (And it kinda does.)

Mercury
Heavily cratered from the impacts of everyone else's bullshit that it didn't ask for.

Venus
This planet deals with 92 times more pressure than Earth does. So, like, lay off.

Earth
It can't stop vaping those greenhouse gases.

Mars
Just because it has the potential to host, doesn't mean it's really going to.

Jupiter
Radiates more energy than it receives.

Saturn
Keeps personal boundaries.

Uranus
Was the butt of a lot of jokes in middle school. Always orbiting somewhere far off in the distance.

Neptune
It got cast out from where everyone else is hanging out, and it's blue about it.

Pluto
Treated like a second-class citizen in its own solar system!

Pluto, babe, you're totally valid to us.

QUEER OUTER SPACE

Asteroids
The "leftovers" of the solar system that just cannot stop moving.

Comets
People are constantly calling them names they haven't consented to.

Plasma
Responsible for the colorful light show. Known as a "new" state of matter even though it's been around literally forever.

Super Clusters
Hang out in like-minded groups with similar interests.

Stars
Will eventually make this all about the zodiac.

Galaxies
Often seen spiraling.

Black Holes
Massive stars can leave quite an impact when they die.

Cosmic Voids
These vast areas without much activity really need their space away from the masses. Far, far away.

Space Junk
Travels at high speeds, and even the smallest ones can do some major damage.

Solar Flares
Have sudden, unpredictable bursts of energy.

Nebulas
Are always in the know when new stars are born.

Space Dust
It's ketamine.

Supernovae
They party so hard right before they die that they blind entire galaxies.

A supernova isn't going down without a serious bender.

Serving Conclusions

→ **LGBTQ+ aliens also cut their own hair in the bathroom.**
→ **Stephen Hawqueen is an icon.**
→ **We have a lot in common with Pluto.**

PART 2

Social Sciences

Science isn't just about gay organisms, it's about how those organisms do gay things to one another! Gay social science helps us understand our community, the rules we make for ourselves, and how we speak to one another, queen. These upcoming fields will address gay human behavior but won't take responsibility for it.

Anthropology
Learn about the evolution of the DIY lesbian subtype and why Disney gays are outsmarting the rest of us.

Education
Your mom definitely experimented in college. Was that just a college thing?

History
There's a rich and fascinating history behind the gay male harness.

Law
If lesbians ran the world, what would our Supreme Court look like?

Linguistics
Discover the impact that trans people have had on language, and review other fascinating trans inventions.

Demography
Become familiar with open relationships and their impact on gay demographics.

Psychology
It's not just you, some same-gender couples do look like twins, and there's a scientific reason behind the doppelbänger phenomenon.

Communication Studies
That girly handwriting is a dead giveaway that you're gay. Explore why!

Sociology
Educate yourself on the gay social order, learn what it means to be intersex, and get acquainted with the pansexual cost-benefit analysis.

Criminology
This one's all about gay crime and punishment. Dostoe-yas queen!

Are Vers-Bottoms Going Extinct?

The Tea: Save the vers-bottoms!

Get PrEPared

You'll learn how to:

✔ **Compare and contrast** sexual positions

✔ **Identify** 10 extinct gay subtypes

✔ **Understand** what a "side" is

Why it's important:

✔ We should be cautious to avoid a Gay Matrix.

A Depression Prediction

In 1997, renowned anthropologist turned-singer-songwriter **Dr. Paula Cole** asked us the burning question: "Where have all the cowboys gone?" Having researched the reduction of biodiversity in gay male subtypes, she was warning us about the endangered nature of **vers-bottoms**.

But society missed the warning call as heterosexuals mistook this as commentary on the failing Dallas Cowboys, who would never see the same Super Bowl success of the early '90s. We don't know what any of that means, but we do know about gay sex!

Not Just Tops and Bottoms

A few centuries ago, gay men weren't stereotyped by just a handful of sexual positions like top, bottom, and vers. They were stereotyped by thousands of them! The rich diversity of labels on sexual preferences benefited our community with better self-expression, robust economic opportunities, and more interesting sex parties.

Soon, many gay subtype roles like clockwise, counterclockwise, and longitudinal were finding themselves vulnerable to extinction.

Extinct Gay Positions

Forward	Longitudinal
Backward	Retrograde
Windward	Perpendicular
Leeward	Parallel
Starboard	Subterranean
Port	Hitherward
Clockwise	Thitherward
Counterclockwise	Witherward
Inward	To and Fro
Outward	Circumsolar
Peripheral	Orbital
Transverse	Criss-cross

FAGTOID!

When the United Slaytions noticed a downward global trend in gay sexual position diversity, they voted on creating a new subtype to add variety: the "side" (no anal). Most gay scientists don't classify this as a true identifier, as most sides are just bottoms who are too lazy to douche.

Homo-glomerate

Like corporate mergers, the consolidation of position types lacked proper congressional oversight. As types died off, the community was left with the three you see today (top, vers, bottom) and two sub-subtypes in between them (vers-top, vers-bottom). Even worse, scientists project that vers-bottoms will be fully extinct by 2050.

PROJECTED SUBTYPE BIOAVAILABILITY

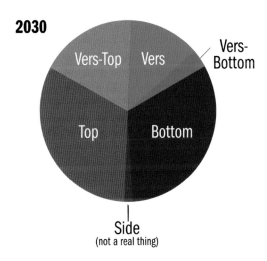

2030

There are two main reasons for this:

Actual Extinction

Vers-bottoms have been going back in the closet. Because they are a vulnerable subtype due to their submissive nature, they succumb to pressures like religion and conversion therapy whenever they are exposed to them. Many vers-bottoms can sustain a closeted relationship with a woman because there's just enough top in them to make it through another day with her.

Perceived Extinction

The vers-bottoms that remain endure a type of bottom-shaming called **bottomism**. To many, topping a top sounds hot, but bottoming for a bottom sounds disgusting. This double standard leaves vers-bottoms feeling less desired, so they have shifted to self-identifying as either bottoms or vers.

With so few vers-bottoms left, most scientists agree that the subtype will totally die out by 2050, leading the way to further divide the gay order into increasingly strict roles. Without much competition in this new binary, there is a theory that tops will fully control bottoms, similar to how sentinels controlled humans in the film *The Matrix*.

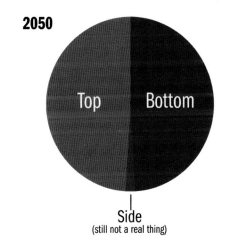

2050

Serving Conclusions

→ **Vers-bottoms are the giant pandas of the gay community.**

→ **Yes, we made a reference to the Dallas Cowboys, and no, we won't do it again.**

Will Bottoms Survive the Apocalypse?

The Tea: The gay after tomorrow is coming.

Get PrEPared

You'll learn how to:

✔ **Understand** the difference between the six major extinctions

✔ **Identify** which gays will die first

✔ **Recognize** why gays always carry cash

✔ **Memorize** soft choreography

Why it's important:

✔ You need to start making the right friends now, before it's too late.

What Is Mass Extinction?

A mass extinction is nature's way of doing a hard reset when things get lame. Earth is the host of this party, and if it hates its own guest list, it's only a matter of time before it kills them all at once, without warning. There have been five major mass extinctions in history, and we're currently living in the sixth one, the **Heterogene Extinction**. Though the gay community has tried to alarm the world about this catastrophe, it's simply too late now.

Since they're often depicted as weak and needy, will bottoms be the first to go? We'll get to that, but first, let's explore the mass extinctions that have happened up to this point.

History of Extinction

Now:

The Heterogene Extinction
This is happening right now. (Sorry, sis!)

66 Million Years Ago:

Cretaceous-Paleogene Extinction
An asteroid struck Earth and killed three-quarters of all life. Triceratops died because there were no tricerabottoms.

201 Million Years Ago:

Triassic-Jurassic Extinction
Volcanic eruptions in the Central Atlantic Magmatic Province killed 35 percent of marine life and most reptiles. It was so C.A.M.P.

252 Million Years Ago:

Permian-Triassic Extinction
The largest known mass extinction was also called "The Great Dying," which was not as fierce as it sounds.

370 Million Years Ago:

Late Devonian Extinction
This extinction knocked out full coral reef systems, sponges, and other really chill and DL marine bacteria.

445 Million Years Ago:

Ordovician Extinction
In the second largest mass extinction, we lost a lot of brachiopods and trilobites. We googled what these looked like, and to be honest, we're totally okay with this extinction.

THE 6 EXTINCTION PERIODS

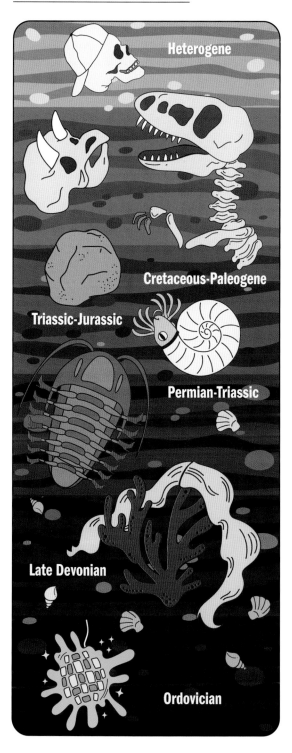

Heterogene

Cretaceous-Paleogene

Triassic-Jurassic

Permian-Triassic

Late Devonian

Ordovician

The Heterogene Extinction

Also known as the *Barstool Sports extinction*, our sixth mass extinction has been triggered by too much manmade heterosexual activity. All this straight nonsense has made our animals and living species so uncomfortable they are offing themselves at an alarming rate. The lack of biodiversity will kill humans soon enough, but not all at once. So, which gays will survive?

A dodo bird ended its existence after experiencing human heterosexuality.

Gay Order of Extinction

There is a predicted order that details which gay people will die first. Note: *lesbians* will have already left Earth and built a utopia on another planet.

First to die: **log cabin gays** These gay Republicans probably caused this mess, and besides, they're dead inside already. We'll also probably see the death of *Bravo gays, astrology gays,* and *tops.* The *plant gays* and *horror-genre gays* will have a decent chance of survival. But most likely to survive are the *bottoms.*

In multiple simulations, bottoms survived a mass extinction 99.8 percent of the time. In the 0.2 percent of scenarios where bottoms did pass away, they died from thirst, even though they had plenty of water. There are three qualities that make them extra fit for survival: resourcefulness, fitness, and knowledge.

A bottom without tops, dying of thirst.

Bottom Survival Qualities

Resourcefulness

Prepared for anything, a bottom will always travel with a backpack that's full of everything they might ever need.

WHAT'S INSIDE A BOTTOM'S BACKPACK?

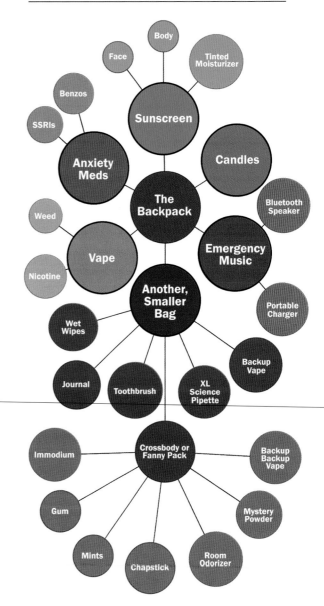

A bottom packs multiple candles.

A bottom will have a bag for everything.

Fitness

Pop singers who can't really dance will often integrate **soft choreography** into their routines. Supported by background dancers and a lighting quick edit, these simple arm and leg movements give the appearance of actual choreography. Soft choreography works very specific muscle groups that are perfect in a doomsday scenario, and gays have been studying these moves since adolescence.

Dua Lipa Hip Twist

Hip flexor choreography assists in moving through fallen debris, cracks, and crevices.

Lohands

These Lindsay Lohan hand movements signal **bottom status**, so they can ditch the tops to survive.

The Hilary Duff Forearm Shield

Prevents foreign debris from entering the eyes when hit with unpredicted high winds.

The Mandy Moore Hard Lip Sync

Works every single muscle of the face, which helps with nonverbal communication when avoiding evil AI regimes.

Avril Thumb Diss

Useful when you need to tell competing bottom scavengers, "Scoot! This is our territory."

The Jessica Simpson Arm Toss

Reminds survivors of Jessica Simpson's existence to give them mental strength.

<u>Knowledge</u>

Bottoms have the highest completion rate of the **Gay Scouts program**, an institution that's over 100 years old. This program teaches adult queer men how to live their best lives and avoid the threat of heterosexuality.

Most bottoms have achieved the highest rank from Piglet to Daddy and have earned the essential merit badges that will help them in a disaster.

GAY SCOUT MERIT BADGES

Bear Culture
Teaches scouts how to identify bears and catch certain bear migrations, like Folsom.

Emergency Preparedness
Teaches scouts how to douche in a nontraditional setting or survive a nude leak.

Heterosexual Survival Scenarios
Provides knowledge on how to survive work-related happy hours or how to complete an errand with Dad without being called a slur.

Catfish Spotting
Helps scouts learn about different types of Internet catfish and how to spot them.

Bottom-on-Bottom Crime Prevention
Helps scouts stop B-o-B crime before it happens in their community.

Open Relationship Navigation
Helps scouts identify different types of open couples.

Cum
Teaches scouts about cum management and cum first aid.

Citizenship in a Gay City
Provides a scout with the info they need to make their city gayer.

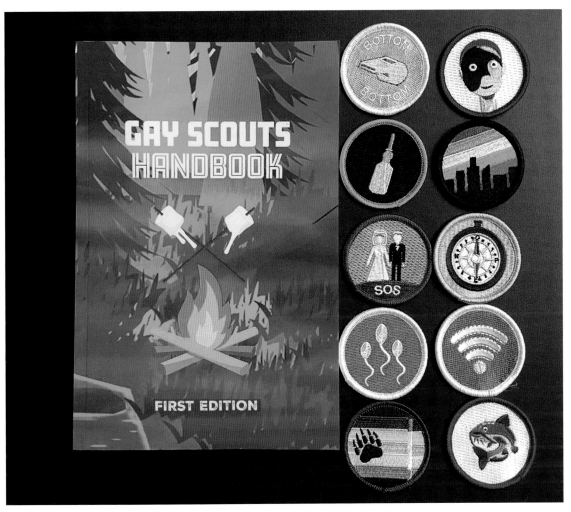

The *Gay Scouts Handbook* will help you obtain Gay Scout Merit Badges.

FAGTOID!

The Gay Scout Oath:
On my honor I will do my best to do my duty to pop culture in my country and obey the Gay Scout Law; to support Britney at all times; to keep myself mentally strong, always awake, and never straight.

Serving Conclusions

→ **A bottom isn't overpacking. They're just preparing for the apocalypse.**

→ **Gays vape.**

→ **A good gay must support Britney at all times.**

The DIY Lesbian, Explained

The Tea: Inside every DIY lesbian is a magnetic stud finder.

Get PrEPared

You'll learn how to:

✔ **Compare** different DIY lesbians

✔ **Understand** how DIY lesbians evolved over time

Why it's important:

✔ There's a serious connection between a lesbian and her projects.

Doing It Themselves

At a home-improvement store, you'll find drywall panels, wall plates, dehumidifiers, and at least one lesbian on cloud nine. This is the do-it-yourself (DIY) lesbian, an exceptional homosexual type that has evolved to be her own designer, landscaper, HVAC subcontractor, furniture maker, electrician, and WD-40 savant.

Yes, a **DIY lesbian** made that rug with her own tufting gun, but she also made the yarn too: spun from hemp she gathered at a queer co-op garden. But the DIY type isn't just exclusive to home projects. There are many other subtypes and sub-subtypes:

DIY LESBIAN NOMENCLATURE

Sub-subtype	Subtype	Type	Letter
Oil Painting	Artistic		
Bird House Building			
Clay Molding			
Nook Making			
Epoxy Pouring			
Garden-Focused	Environmental	DIY	Lesbian
Repurposing			
Composting			
Upcycling			
Beekeeping			
Thrift Hauling	Economical		
Corner Cutting			
Cheap-as-Fuck			

Why Do Lesbians DIY?

Repurposing

Somewhere, right now, a DIY lesbian is saving wine corks to make a portrait of Tracy Chapman with them. Giving "trash" a second life makes a gay girl feel like she's getting the full value out of a product, and scientists have found that each upcycled project adds another six months onto a lesbian's life.

Scarlett O'Hara's dress made from green curtains was DIY lesbian-coded.

Originality

When a lesbian fires up a handmade ceramic bird bath in the kiln, she becomes the only person in the world with *that* bird bath. There's a power in that. When you DIY, your life is custom. DIY lesbians are living custom-made lives in which they are the designers.

Dexterity

We would trust a DIY lesbian's hands with our lives.

Control

DIY lesbians like to gauge a project's difficulty based on their own experiences. They enjoy taking responsibility for its outcome, whether it's a success or failure. If the **catio** construction was a total flop, then at least *they* were the ones who fucked it up.

Cat patios are DIY lesbian culture.

Serving Conclusions

→ **Lesbians are good with their hands.**
→ **She'll never give up on the catio.**

Disney Gays, Explained

The Tea: Disney gays know something you don't know.

Get PrEPared

You'll learn how to:
✔ **Understand** the appeal of Disney
✔ **Reconsider** which brands to value

Why it's important:
✔ Corporate adoption day is coming.

What Is a Disney Gay?

Did you know there are adult LGBTQ+ people that are fully devoted to Disney? Collectables line the shelves of their homes. They blow out Lumière candles on their birthdays. They get Mickey Mouse tattoos (and later get sued for infringement). When you see a Disney gay post on social media about their 1,000th visit to a Disney park, you may be asking yourself: "Aren't they too old for this?" First, mind your business. Second, we'll explain.

A Disney gay getting his endorphins back.

Escapism

The transition into adulthood can be a rough go for some of the LGBTQ+. To cope, they hold on to memories from childhood and try to permanently live in them. Escapism is why we see adults using coloring books, making friendship bracelets, hosting tea parties in Provincetown and Fire Island, or playing dress-up. People don't seem to pass as much judgment here as they do with Disney gays, who have actually chosen the most robust coping mechanism with its multiple film franchises, television shows, Broadway musicals, theme parks, and cruises.

Environment

If you're a gay man living in Orlando, Tampa, or Daytona Beach, what else are you gonna do?

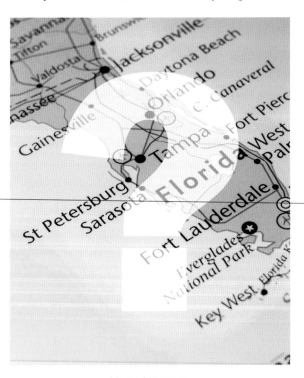

It's one big swamp.

Corporate Pledging

In the future, six corporations will own all human beings in the United States: Apple, Google, Amazon, Meta, Disney, and Waffle House.

The Giant Hole.

Citizens pledging to the Big Six.

Humans without corporate sponsors will not have the means to provide for themselves and will be thrown into The Giant Hole. Disney gays are placing their bets on Disney and showing their allegiance early and often to ensure they are chosen and provided for when the corporate adoption day comes on **July 2, 2038**.

A Disney Gay Explains

DISNEY DECOR

Look, I'm not saying Disney decor isn't weird, but you do know that some people hang the carcasses of dead animals on their walls for decoration, right?

Serving Conclusions

➡ **What do you even do in Daytona Beach?**

➡ **There are worse things to be than a Disney gay, so, like, chill.**

Why Are Gay Boys Always the Female Teacher's Favorite?

The Tea: See me after class (so we can spill).

Get PrEPared

You'll learn how to:

✔ **Identify** four reasons why gay boys are the favorites

✔ **Understand** why gay boys are creative

Why it's important:

✔ A gay kid has special powers in the classroom.

What's the hot goss in the teacher's lounge?

You should put an Olivia Rodrigo vinyl in the prize box. The class would eat that up.

Did you watch *Vanderpump Rules*?

I can't believe they make you pay for school supplies . . . hopefully you write that off, bestie.

The Gay Boys Just Get It

Ask any female teacher who she fangirls over the most in her classroom and she will always identify one person: the gay boy. Female educators appreciate the way young fruity brains are built. Here are four reasons why:

Emotional Intelligence

Homosexual boys are drawn to women leaders like sailors to a siren. While most kids are ready to bolt from a class when the bell rings, gay boys hang around and get on the teacher's level.

They initially build trust by pointing out frustrating school system issues that she deals with every day, while also becoming a safe space for backchat. Here are some of the things you might hear a gay boy say to his female teacher:

Teachers often feel more valued and appreciated by their gay students in class than they do by their own husbands.

"That gay kid really gets me."

Responsibility

When a straight boy takes the class pet rabbit home for the weekend, it will come back with missing fur and a broken leg.

When a gay boy takes the rabbit home, it will return to class with a fresh carrot oil skin treatment while smelling of Le Labo. It's newly remodeled enclosure will feature an accessible bunny ramp, mid-century modern furniture with matching decor, a designer salt lick, and filtered Brita water sitting inside a stainless steel bottle with a buy-one-give-one model. For every rabbit water bottle you buy, one is given to a rabbit in need!

Mrs. Donovan's class is on their fifth pet rabbit this year. She has no gay boys in her class.

A class rabbit after homosexual care.

Deferred Romance

As the straight students become distracted passing notes to their crushes, many gay boys don't have that option yet and pay more attention to their school work.

Creativity

This Thanksgiving, most of the class drew a shitty turkey on the outline of their hands, but the gay kid made an entire scene at a turkey farm around his, with one turkey being given the special distinction of being pardoned by the president.

And the hands of that turkey have been drawn to look like mini turkeys. And they, too, have been pardoned by presidents. Their own mini presidents.

Serving Conclusions

→ **When it comes to being heard, gay boys > your husband.**

→ **The straight boys should lose their class pet privileges.**

Does College Make People Bi?

The Tea: We're just experimenting.

Bi-formation

Are universities so woke they're turning people bi? Why does everyone decide to experiment while they're in college? If you never attend college, can you ever come out? College is indeed a breeding ground for bisexuality. These students are quite likely to experiment with someone of a new sex, especially after a few rounds of beer pong. However, the notion that faculty have an "agenda" to expose students to a new sexuality is fully bogus. They actually have an entire curriculum! If you don't believe us, just ask your parents.

YOUR DAD IN COLLEGE, PROBABLY:

"A mouth is a mouth."

Now let's examine the three main influences behind collegiate bisexual conversion:

Isolated Environment

If you mix 18-year-old hormones with no parental oversight, you're gonna end up with some horny students. Collect them together in one place, and they'll find fewer gender hang-ups than they would otherwise.

ISOLATED ENVIRONMENTS MOST LIKELY TO TURN YOU BI

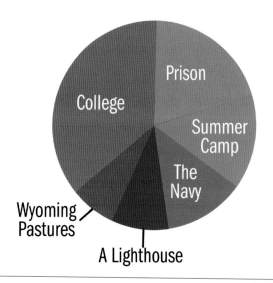

Prison
College
Summer Camp
The Navy
Wyoming Pastures
A Lighthouse

Hotter Population

A new college student is more likely to be attracted to multiple genders in college because the pool of people just got *way* more intelligent and attractive, as compared to their hometown clowns. When everyone gets hotter, things become more bisexual.

Mary is relieved she will never have to sleep with another man in her hometown.

Your bisexual nemesis on his way to fuck your brother *and* your sister.

A Bisexual (Your Mom) Explains

COLLEGE

Hey, sweetie, it's Mom! Love that you're getting a good gay education. I think it's probably time to let you know that, in college, before I met your father I used to eat out literally all my girlfriends! I couldn't get enough. I also basically sucked off the entire campus. Before you get all weird, it was a small liberal arts school, so there weren't that many students! But, yeah, I was an insatiable bisexual! But now I'm just a regular bisexual and very proud to be your mom.

Enlightenment

Being in an institution of higher learning, it's natural for young people to reach greater planes of awareness. Opening their minds, they find more creative interpretations to themed parties, embrace sleeping anywhere, and begin to understand that bisexual people are doing it better. They benefit from:

- **Living in the largest dating pool possible**
- **Having more porn to watch**
- **Sexual preferences within a relationship staying consistent even if one partner transitions**
- **No longer needing to change the pronouns in songs**
- **Unlimited bi pun potential**
- **Fucking every member of your enemies' families**
- **A special power of invisibility**

Serving Conclusions

→ **Colleges are full of bisexuals.**

→ **College kids will fuck anything.**

→ **Your mom was such an icon in college.**

Are LGBTQ+ People Responsible for All These Hurricanes?

The Tea: What did we do this time?

Get PrEPared

You'll learn how to:
- ✔ **Identify** seven LGBTQ+ storms
- ✔ **Identify** five different types of gay hurricanes

Why it's important:
- ✔ A gay hurricane could hit at any time.

What Causes a Storm?

Conservatives and religious figures are always blaming the LGBTQ+ Gazebo for something. In 2017, right-wingers blamed "transgender bathrooms" for a flood in California. That same year they also blamed trans people for Hurricane Harvey. And in 2015, trans people created **Rachel Dolezal**, apparently. According to an Italian academic, gays caused the fall of Rome. But it was a US Christian radio host who blamed the financial crisis of 2008 on a "prosodomy Gestapo." Yes, a subprime mortgage fallout caused by anal-sex Nazis.

Are storms and natural disasters created when people of the same sex get married or when transgender people do transgender things? Of course they are! Let's look at the different kinds of storms LGBTQ+ people create:

Bi Blizzard

Occurs when an event draws a significant increase in bisexual attendance. You'll know it's a bi blizzard because you can hear the sounds of keychains jangling, since bisexuals carry at least two dozen keys on their carabiners at all times.

Gay Cyclone

Created when a group of gay friends enter your vicinity and all of them look identical.

Lesbian Squall

A sudden, sharp increase in lesbian energy that typically results from a lesbian love triangle.

Trans Tornado

Caitlyn Jenner ruining everything.

Firestorm

When the word gets out that you have a house on Fire Island this holiday weekend, so all the **day trippers** ask to crash there.

Gay Flood

This happens after a vacation destination has been "made gay" on social media and everyone starts booking their flights for next year.

Gay Hurricane

Not just one, but a collection of trends that occur when gays weasel their way into society. The rest of this chapter will explore the historical progress of same-sex unions and how they align with gay hurricanes.

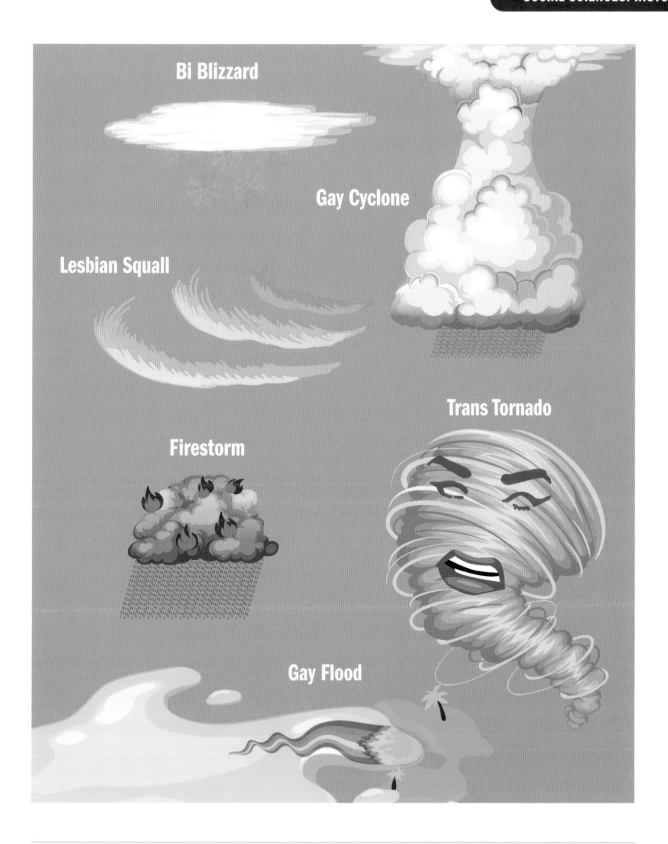

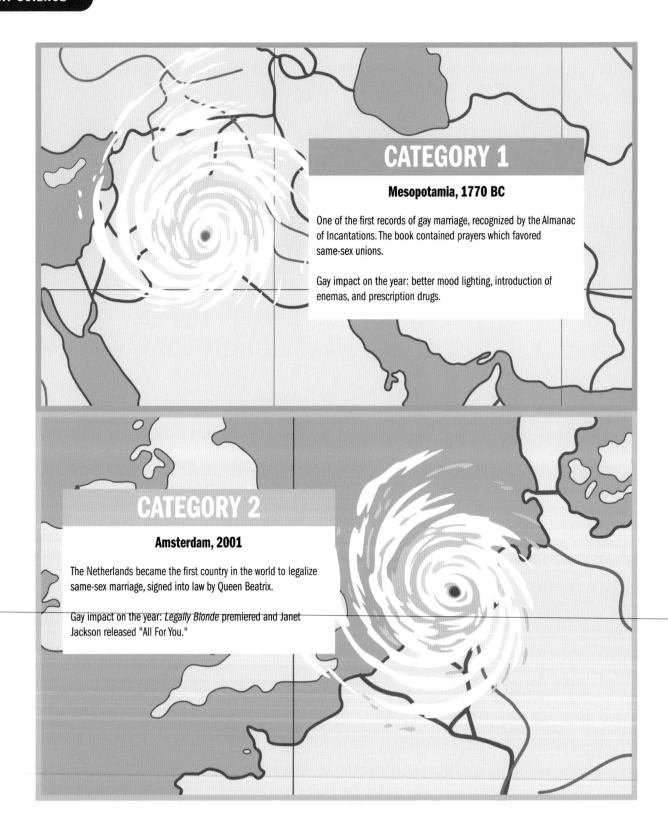

CATEGORY 1

Mesopotamia, 1770 BC

One of the first records of gay marriage, recognized by the Almanac of Incantations. The book contained prayers which favored same-sex unions.

Gay impact on the year: better mood lighting, introduction of enemas, and prescription drugs.

CATEGORY 2

Amsterdam, 2001

The Netherlands became the first country in the world to legalize same-sex marriage, signed into law by Queen Beatrix.

Gay impact on the year: *Legally Blonde* premiered and Janet Jackson released "All For You."

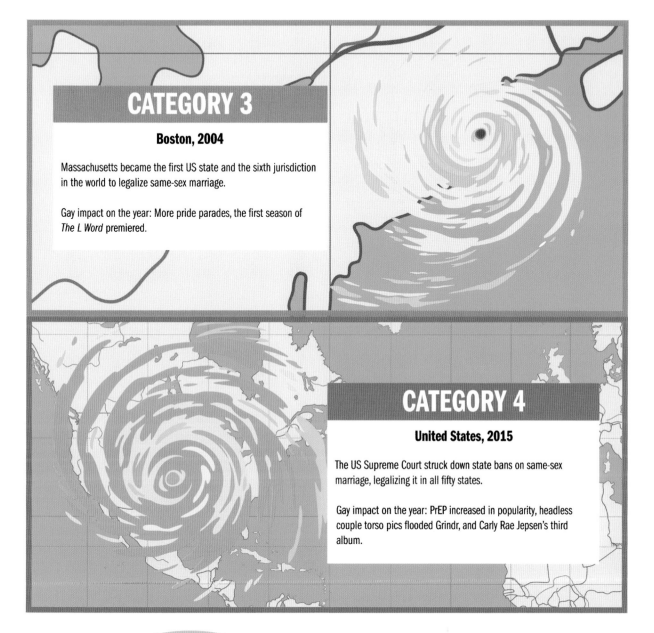

CATEGORY 3

Boston, 2004

Massachusetts became the first US state and the sixth jurisdiction in the world to legalize same-sex marriage.

Gay impact on the year: More pride parades, the first season of *The L Word* premiered.

CATEGORY 4

United States, 2015

The US Supreme Court struck down state bans on same-sex marriage, legalizing it in all fifty states.

Gay impact on the year: PrEP increased in popularity, headless couple torso pics flooded Grindr, and Carly Rae Jepsen's third album.

FAGTOID!

During the Han Dynasty, almost all emperors were in same-sex unions. Can you guess where silk robes and handheld fans came from?

Serving Conclusions

→ **What are bisexuals doing with all those keys?**

→ **Zipolite had a gay flood.**

Why Do Gay Men Wear Harnesses?

The Tea: A leather daddy is always ready to rappel.

Get PrEPared

You'll learn how to:

✔ **Identify** who invented the harness

✔ **Understand** why gay men wear harnesses

Why it's important:

✔ Honestly, we're not really sure it is.

What Are Those Straps For?

If you took a field trip to the **Folsom Street Fair** in San Francisco, you'd find plenty of gay men wearing a few straps of leather or fabric across their bare chests and torsos. These are harnesses! Why are they wearing them, though? Did they just wash the windows of a high-rise building? Are they going bungee jumping later?

The harness is a medical device that improves the quality of life for circuit queens and other homosexuals across the globe. Harnesses have evolved over time and are worn for many different reasons!

A gay man talks to his health insurance provider about covering the cost of a harness.

Three men about to rappel.

A man wearing his medical device.

The First Harness

The earliest form of the harness was seen in the Roman Colosseum. When homosexual gladiators were given their fighting outfits, they thought the armor was hiding all the work they'd been putting in on their bodies. The solution was a strap across the chest that connected lighter pieces of armor that could show off their bench press results. Though this apparel decision proved to be a fatal one, they still looked hot while dying.

So bulky.

So sexy.

FAGTOID!
Hot, dying gay gladiators in harnesses revived the Colosseum industry.

A Nordic Inventor

In early 20th-century Helsinki, **Thomas of Finland**, a young tannery-worker-slash-policeman, created the first authentic homosexual harness. He noticed that gays were possessed with an affliction of involuntarily removing their shirts at any place, for whatever reason, at any hour of the day. Tired of seeing his friends thrown out of Finnish establishments over their condition, he created a series of leather straps to be placed over the shirt to prevent the gay from removing it, and called it *hihna päällä*, or strap on.

Gay men eventually found many other uses for the harness, some even saving lives.

Thomas of Finland was known for his impeccable leatherwork and policing.

Harnesses became a great way to keep tabs on wandering partners.

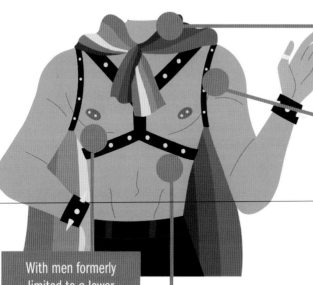

Distracted boyfriends used to wear collars to prevent them from wandering away at social functions, but these were swapped for harnesses after a few ended up with snapped necks.

In the unlikely occurrence that the homosexual's muscles decide to suddenly detach themselves, this will hold them in place until they can be reattached.

With men formerly limited to a lower weight-carrying capacity, the harness allowed them to bear more loads.

A harness is as close as some gay men will ever get to receiving a good hug.

Serving Conclusions

→ **It's homophobic that this medical device isn't FSA eligible.**

→ **Finland is so gay for this.**

→ **That guy in the harness just took so many loads.**

GAY EXPERIMENT

Make Your Own Harness at Home!

Take your DIY skills to the next level! Learn how to repurpose your old gay striped bowling shirt into a hot new harness.

LEVEL OF DIFFICULTY: HIGH | **LEVEL OF GAY:** VERY | **TIME SUGGESTION:** 60 MINUTES

Materials

- The striped gay shirt sitting in your closet right now
- Fabric scissors
- Thin black marker

The Steps

1. Take the striped gay shirt that you bought from Zara in 2019 out of your closet. If you own multiple (you probably do, queen) then you'll have a few backups if you mess up.
2. Choose a harness style that suits your body. This is a great chance to cover up a scar or bad tattoo!
3. Use the marker to outline the strap design. Remember to include at least one button connection in your outline.
4. Cut along the inside of the marker outline.
5. Wear your harness proudly (unless you're in a small, Southern town or something).

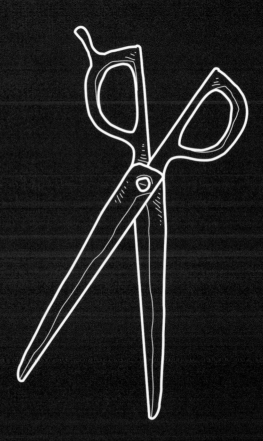

NOW TRY THIS!

Once you've mastered this, try different fabrics! Get creative with curtains, bed sheets, and tote bags!

A New Queer World, Examined: What if the Gays Were in Charge?

The Tea: Hint: Subarus are involved.

Get PrEPared

You'll learn how to:

✔ **Understand** why the LGBTQ+ population is growing

✔ **Visualize** how gays and lesbians would run the world

Why it's important:

✔ This will be our future so you might as well prepare for it now.

Are the LGBTQ+ Taking Over?

Over 7 percent of people in the United States consider themselves part of the alphabet mafia, double what it was 10 years ago. How is this possible?

Dr. Paula Abdul, a leading researcher in the field of **vibeology**, determined that heterosexual population growth didn't pass the vibe check, as this sharp **J-curve** was hitting planet Earth in the wrong spots. And without any lube!

Dr. Abdul checking vibes.

Population Growth

Dresses with peekaboo shoulders. Dog names like "Charlie" or "Bella." Men with Samurai swords hanging on the wall. The Earth has reached its carrying capacity for heteronormativity, and all this straight behavior has Mother at a breaking point.

HETEROSEXUAL POPULATION GROWTH

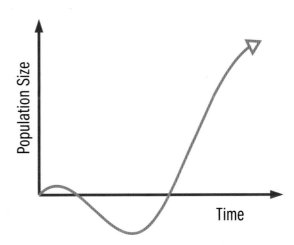

The LGBTQ+ started multiplying to save the world, and because they aren't heavy reproducers, the only answer was recruitment. Each year they distribute a queer census to measure recruitment activities. This is distributed in collector's editions of the '90s sitcom *Absolutely Fabulous* and digitally on the Co-Star app.

Civics Sisters

But what if it didn't have to be this way? What if gay men ran this thing from the start? What if lesbians were in the driver's seat? Let's examine a new gay country!

A NEW QUEER WORLD, RUN BY:

	Gays	Lesbians
Constitution	Starts as a serious thing, then becomes just a thread of memes.	Written in the form of a poem. Any amendments to the constitution are presented to a live slam poetry audience.
Taxes	Replaced with a massive, cash-only cover charge, though most everyone knows at least one guy in the IRS and doesn't have to pay it.	Two-week relationships living in the same household are given the same tax breaks as marriages.
Elections and Voting	All candidates must release their nudes.	No one can vote until Mercury is out of retrograde.
States	We have 50 states, but everyone just crams into one or two.	Every person gets their own state.
Transportation	Government-funded.	Only Subarus.
Military	All military workouts are live-streamed.	This Pentagon passes their audits.
Law Enforcement	Uniforms only have buttons midway down.	Miranda Rights = the right to turn sapphic in the reboot.
Economy	Every citizen has a side business. But no one knows how to budget for a business correctly.	In addition to receiving sick and vacation days, letter-writing days are also included in PTO.
Immigration	If the top/bottom balance is out of order, the oversupplied type wait longer to get a visa.	Difficult for lesbian psychologists and sociologists to immigrate (too many already).
Religion	Religion is classified as Munchausen's syndrome by proxy.	The zodiac.
Health	The major pharmaceutical companies also manufacture party drugs.	Zoloft dispensers are readily available across all major cities.
Education	John Waters cinema studies is required learning.	Because lesbians love having milestones, grades K-8 are replaced with "milestones."

What Would the Different LGBTQ+ Government Branches Look Like?

Legislative Branch

There would be four different chambers for each core letter (LGBT), expanding to 11 chambers (LGBTQQIP2SA), and eventually anyone could self-identify as their own sexuality and become a chamber of one.

At the end of a legislative session, the gay chamber would host an afters, to which they would arrive late.

Executive Branch

The president would always be a woman, and we'd call her Mother. Here's what her gay cabinet could look like:

- **Madam President (Mother)**
- **Vice President (Stepmom/Stepdad)**
- **Secretary of Stating Facts**
- **Secretary of Verbal Conjecture**
- **Attorney Generally Late**
- **Secretary of the Interior Design**
- **Secretary of Watering the Plants While I'm Gone**
- **Secretary of Never in Labor**
- **Secretary of Prophylaxis**
- **Secretary of Gender-Affirming Care**
- **Secretary of Housing and Urban Redecoration**
- **Secretary of Vacation Transportation**
- **Secretary of Dog Meetups**
- **Secretary of Hyperbolic Affairs**
- **Fan Fiction Protection Agency**
- **Director of Zoloft Distribution**

Judicial Branch

Courtroom judges would be replaced with four talent-show judges who would hold up score cards to be tallied to determine total sentencing.

Here's who would be the Supreme Court:

- **Kelly Clarkson**
- **Niecy Nash**
- **Patti LuPone**
- **Maya Rudolph**
- **RuPaul**
- **Ina Garten**
- **Xena, Warrior Princess**
- **Ms. Frizzle from *The Magic School Bus***
- **A rotating cast of witches**

Judges totally serving (the maximum sentence).

Serving Conclusions

→ **Everyone in the gay military also has an OnlyFans.**

→ **Government-funded Lexapro dispensers are a queer dream come true.**

→ **Milestones are lesbian-coded.**

Why Do Gay Men Talk Like That?

The Tea: There's no hiding that voice, queen.

That's a (Gay) Man, Maury

You know it instantly: that high-pitched voice with a trill is coming from a gay man. **Gay voice** is one of the most recognizable sounds on the planet. Some linguists say you're hearing an example of assibilation, while others owe the sound to a fricative, but all agree on one thing: it sure is faggy!

Because they often congregate in earthquake zones, gay men harness a lot of energy. Excess energy that isn't spent relaying local drama passes across the vocal chords to initiate a high-frequency vibration.

(The Hilarious) Ross Matthews is the unofficial spokesman for gay voice. This was the closest stock photo to (The Hilarious) Ross Matthews we could find.

VIBRATION CHART

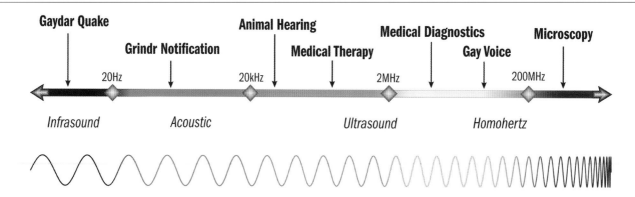

Gaydar Quake — 20Hz — Grindr Notification — Animal Hearing — 20kHz — Medical Therapy — Medical Diagnostics — 2MHz — Gay Voice — Microscopy — 200MHz

Infrasound *Acoustic* *Ultrasound* *Homohertz*

HOMOSEXUALS ON FAULT LINES

Homohertz is a pitch that all people can hear but only gay men (and Dolly Parton) can understand. It provides helpful subtext beyond what's actually being said. This is how gay men read people in public to each other without other people noticing.

Sometimes these high-pitched sounds pass through the mouth into a lisp caused by **fagotta dentata**. This gay voice is an elite form of communication, like echolocation in dolphins, and can transmit sounds up to 10,000 miles away.

Unfortunately, all men are bad listeners, so these messages are lost on them and are exclusively received by Dolly Parton, who's been quietly managing the chaos of hearing the voice of every gay man for decades.

Dolly hears every gay conversation simultaneously.

Serving Conclusions

→ **Men don't listen.**
→ **Homosexuals love impending doom.**
→ **Dolly Parton is a literal saint.**

Did Trans People Invent Pronouns?

The Tea: Pronouns are all fun and games until you misgender someone's dog.

The Great Divider

Myself, anybody, whichever, nobody. These are pronouns! They come in many forms, like possessive, intensive, interrogative, and personal. Sounds just like your ex, right?

Using personal pronouns like *he*, *she*, or *they* is just one way to address someone's gender identity (when you're talking shit about them). Seems simple enough, right? But it might surprise you to learn that all the *she/hers* and *they/thems* on social media profiles have caused some controversy. Opponents of pronouns, called **proponents** (confusingly enough), blame trans and non-binary people for pushing the use of different pronouns upon society. So where did pronouns come from, and why do they infuriate their proponents? (Once again, very confusing.)

The Invention of Pronouns

Trans people started existing only recently. They suddenly appeared out of thin air when American conservatives heard about them on the news for the first time. This is also the case for all minority groups and any topical issues!

Being so new to our world, trans people noticed something weird: the use of language to describe gender identity was pretty limited. Because society only knew how to use proper names and titles, sentences were clunky and flat. People were referring to themselves in the third person!

"Martin Luther King, Jr. has a dream."
—Martin Luther King, Jr. (*pre-pronouns*)

But haven't pronouns always been around?

No! The reason you think this is due to the **Themdela Effect**, similar to the Mandela Effect. Because trans contributions to society have improved human life so greatly, our brains have given us a false collective memory of a world where they didn't exist. You might remember these well-known quotes and lyrics a bit differently, but this is what was originally said:

"Every breath that person takes, every move that person makes, Sting will be watching that person."
—The Police, "Every Breath You Take"

"Toto, Dorothy has a feeling Toto and Dorothy are not in Kansas anymore."
—Dorothy, *The Wizard of Oz*

It's hard to believe people ever dealt with such nonsense in a world without pronouns!

Syntax and Cistax

In addition to changing linguistics forever, trans people have had thousands of words added to the dictionary. Words like *transition* (they used to say "turning from one thing to another thing"), *visibility* (they used to say "able to be seen more"), and *gender* (they used to say "serving vagina/penis").

Trans people also developed semantics so our society could address the meaning behind words and the importance of context, but this concept originally proved too advanced for their critics.

But they/them didn't just stop there! Here are some other trans inventions:

Wigs

New hair quickly and easily? Wig. Avoid being recognized in public? Wig. Who could imagine a world without them?

A beautiful trans contribution.

A beautiful trans contribution.

Trans people can't claim this one, sorry.

Hormones

Before trans people were all like, "Shouldn't we have hormones?" the regulation of metabolism, the reproductive system, and insulin responses were all handled by the government, which meant it took literally forever for people to get what they needed approved.

A life before trans people existed: a three-hour wait to balance your electrolytes.

Public Bathrooms

It was trans people who decided to make public restrooms a thing, which garnered massive support. But then trans people decided to actually use them, which angered their proponents. (You know, they really should consider changing their name.)

A Trans Person Explains

BEING AN INVENTOR

I'm just a really, really bored villain-coded language and pronoun inventor, and not at all just doing the same, normal, routine things everyone else does while trying to live my life with some peace and dignity!

Surgery

No surgeries of any kind had ever been performed until a stunning trans woman said "Do that" to a doctor. Prior to this, doctors used to just spin their patients around really fast or shake them violently to get their pieces back into place.

Serving Conclusions

→ **Your grandpa didn't use pronouns.**

→ **A stunning trans woman really said, "Do that."**

Gay Dating and Open Relationships

The Tea: Calling all emotionally available men!

Get PrEPared

You'll learn how to:

✔ **Understand** why some gay men will be single forever

✔ **Compare** difficult scenarios that occur across gay dating

✔ **Identify** the four types of gay partnerships

Why it's important:

✔ Gay vampires can keep you from finding happiness.

Mating and Dating

Animals date and mate in many different ways. Lovebirds stick close, build elaborate nests, and stay together for life. Flatworms can play male or female and literally have no standards. An

Lovebirds reminding you that you'll never find a love like this.

anglerfish male sinks his teeth into the female and permanently attaches himself to her forever. But dating as a gay male human happens to be the most complicated of all. In terms of difficulty and stress, it is one of the hardest activities one can engage in.

HOW DIFFICULT AND STRESSFUL IS GAY DATING?

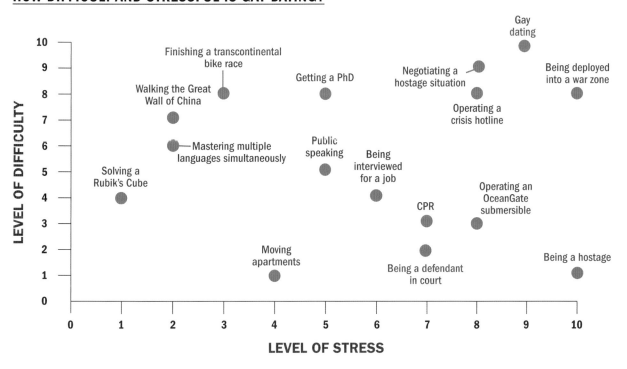

The stress and difficulty of finding a good partner is exponentially increased for gay men because they date within a significantly reduced pool of available men.

GAY DATING POOL

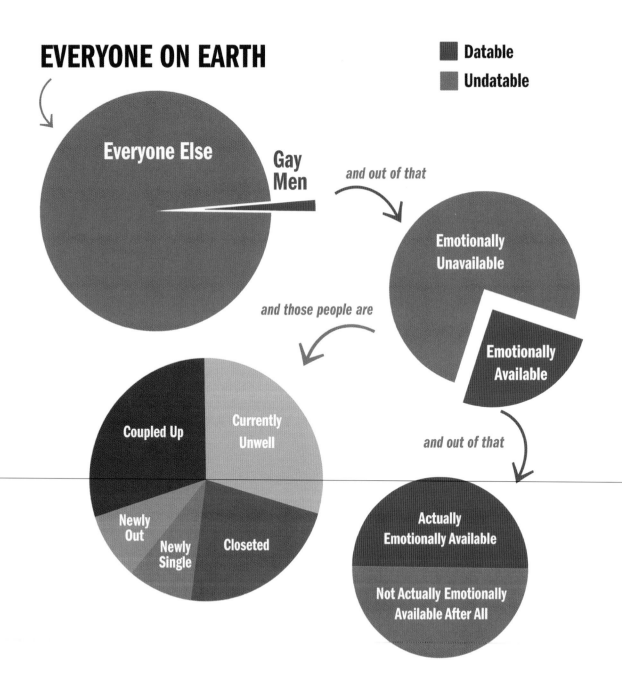

Gay Relationships

Let's look at the unavailable gay men who are already coupled up. If you're thinking it would be hard to categorize many different pairs of people, with their unique experiences and highly specific romantic boundaries, into only a few groups, then you haven't been paying attention to Gay Science. We live for this. There are only four different types of gay partnerships, and nothing more.

OPEN
All partners agree that they can have sexual relations with other people.

ONE-WAY
One partner wants to have sex with other people, and the other is like, "Okay, I guess."

ENDING SOON
Both men agree to have sex with other people five days into dating each other.

CLOSED
All partners agree that they will not have sex with other people, but they probably will anyway.

The Pool

Whether someone is looking for a long-term thing, a one-night stand, or a 10-minute quickie in the woods, single, emotionally available people are the highest quality choice. For those 10 minutes, you're the only person that matters to them. It's usually great sex and it could possibly lead to something even greater. Unfortunately, it's becoming harder to find these types of people.

Gay men suffer from an all-consuming, rapacious disease called **being horny**. They will do anything they want to feel good, especially if they don't have to experience any short-term consequences. Open couples have made this dating pool even smaller twofold. First, by removing themselves from it, and second, by competing for the remaining single men.

OPEN BEHAVIOR

Impact of closed relationships on singles

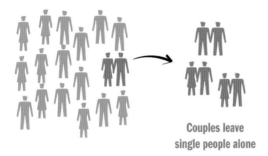

Couples leave
single people alone

Impact of open relationships on singles

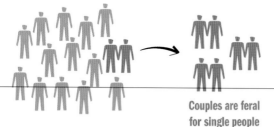

Couples are feral
for single people

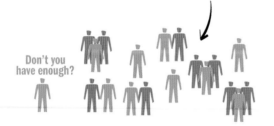

Don't you
have enough?

Driven by the confidence of having nothing to lose, men in open relationships are unmatched aggressors in gay spaces. They are charming, smart, affectionate, and too goddamn hot for their own good.

Unburdened from having to demonstrate the same good communication they do with their partner, they often don't let the single male know their situation until they've already hooked them in and gone home with them. The single male may not find out the guy they've just hooked up with is in an open relationship until they check their Instagram the next morning. By getting tangled up with a guy in an open relationship, the single, emotionally available man has missed out on an opportunity to connect with someone else who could have made his life better.

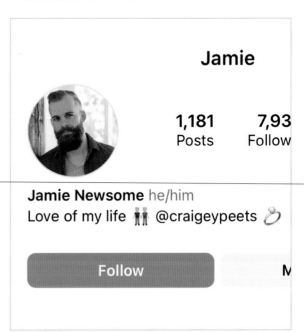

How most men find out that the charming, smart, affectionate, guy they just spent the night with is in an open relationship.

Open Relationship Dynamics and Rules

Open relationships come with rules that are infinite and ever-changing. Single people going home with an open person or open couple may not be told what these rules are. The single person is left with the challenge of determining them by interpreting nonverbal signs and clues from the couple who is about to double penetrate him.

Here are some (but not all) open relationship dynamics the author of this book may have experienced:

When They Play Separately

RULE 101: No hosting.

RULE 102: All hooking up needs to be done at the place you met (bar, club, etc.) and not occur anywhere else.

RULE 110: There is a "no hookup" list established by the couple that predetermines which men their partner is not allowed to hook up with under any circumstances.

RULE 111: There is a "golden ticket" list established by the couple that predetermines which men their partner is allowed to hook up with if they ever get the chance to.

RULE 133: Condoms must always be used.

RULE 134: Okay, condoms don't have to be used, but no one can cum inside.

RULE 142: Can only hook up with other men when the other partner is out of town.

RULE 150: Must tell the other partner about the hookup within 24 hours.

RULE 171: No repeat hookups.

When They Play Together

RULE 201: The third must follow both of them on Instagram, not just the hot one.

RULE 208: No more than one date afterward.

RULE 266: The ancient one who pays all the bills gets to watch.

RULE 270: If one is out of town, they have to Zoom the hookup live.

RULE 288: If one gets your mouth then the other one has to get your eye contact.

RULE 290: They have to hold each other's hands during penetration. They cannot let go until penetration is finished.

A loving gay couple practicing RULE 290 as you enter one of them.

Serving Conclusions

→ Gay dating is about as stressful as being deployed into an active war zone.

→ Open relationships are now everyone's business.

→ Does the weird old guy have to be in the room?

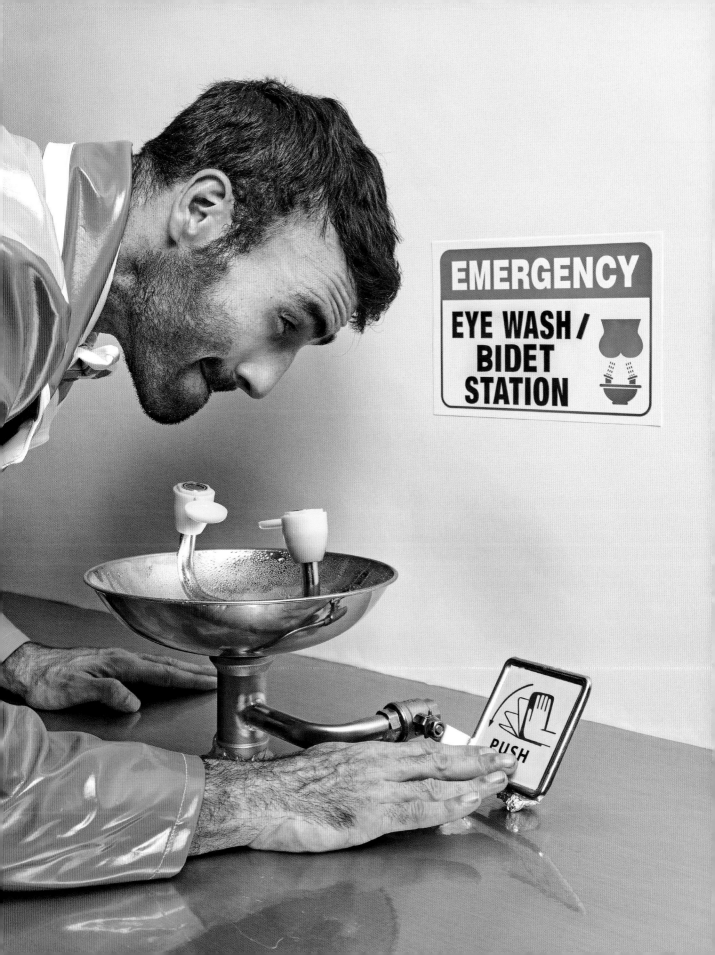

EMERGENCY

EYE WASH /
BIDET
STATION

PUSH

Why Do Gay Men Feel Powerful Immediately After a Haircut?

The Tea: A gay man with a fresh cut? Unstoppable.

Get PrEPared

You'll learn how to:

✔ **Identify** the positive effects of a gay haircut

✔ **Understand** why gay men prefer a fade

Why it's important:

✔ Gay haircut confidence is powerful but temporary, so use it wisely.

The Power of a Haircut

A homosexual will enter a barbershop feeling horrible and leave with the confidence of Beyoncé with a bat. Why does a gay with a fresh cut feel like they can move things with their mind, be best friends with a celebrity, or successfully solve a math problem? It has to do with gay psychology in the form of **homological effects**.

AN ONLOOKER:

"Look at that boy go! He must have just gotten a haircut."

POSITIVE HOMOLOGICAL EFFECTS OF A GAY HAIRCUT

Feeling two inches taller

Looking expensive even though you're broke

Mimicking the feeling of going to the gym without actually going to the gym

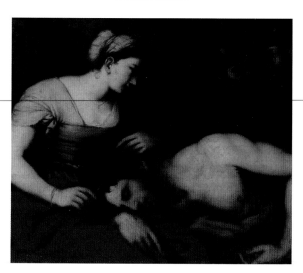

If Samson was gay, Delilah would be doing him a favor.

The Fade

The fade is particularly powerful for gays as it unlocks repressed memories of the first men they were sexually attracted to. Some of these men include:

- **The stars of their high school wrestling team**
- **Performers from classic military or Czech porn**
- **Their best friend's dad**
- **Their own bullies**

Your best friend's dad, probably.

A "drill" sergeant.

Changing the Course of History

But it's not just the perception of power. A study from the **Tanya McQuoid Association of Gay Mortality** shows that major catastrophes have been avoided by the powers that come about because of a gay haircut.

- **Queen Victoria evaded seven assassination attempts by having a secret undercut.**
- **Abraham Lincoln avoided a fatal duel in 1842 by appearing two inches taller after he got a fresh haircut.**
- **No one died at Stonewall because the riots in 1969 happened on a Saturday, and you better believe those gays had gotten a fresh cut on Friday.**

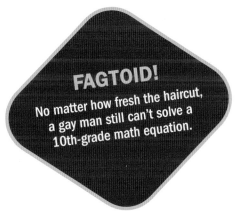

FAGTOID!
No matter how fresh the haircut, a gay man still can't solve a 10th-grade math equation.

Serving Conclusions

→ **Have you been working out or is it just the fade?**
→ **Your best friend's dad was super hot.**

Why Do Gay Men Choose Difficult Vacation Spots?

The Tea: You're going to need an extra day just to get there.

Get PrEPared

You'll learn how to:

✔ **Differentiate** between gay fun and straight fun

✔ **Understand** why gay men isolate themselves from others

Why it's important:

✔ Knowing what a gay vacation spot looks like can help deter (or attract) you.

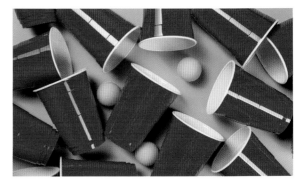

Young straight men will spend an entire night throwing ping pong balls into plastic cups.

Straights love watching a car go in a circle hundreds of times.

Heterosexual card games allow no more than one color printed on them, plus black.

How Straight People Have Fun

Have you ever seen a dog chasing its own tail? It's quite a funny sight! Though it's cute to see a dog find its own source of silly fun, it would be preposterous to assume that you, a human being, would also be entertained by such a daft activity. This is how homosexuals feel when forced to participate in heterosexual pastimes.

For years, homosexuals have been culturally obliged to watch people go back and forth and back and forth and back and forth (what the straights call "sports"), or throw one smaller object at another, bigger object (they call these "lawn games"), or suck smoke into their mouths and swish it around like mouthwash then let it out again (these are "cigars"). If I had a tail, I'd rather just chase that!

Public humiliation, a staple in heterosexual entertainment.

How Gay People Have Fun

While gays occasionally participate in these activities to meet an obligation, too much exposure to these activities may cause the gay to experience a permanent loss of brain function. This ideology also applies to travel. Homosexuals have evolved to add difficulty to their lives so they can weed heterosexuals out of their vacations. The experience of staying in a hotel downtown is not the same thing as staying in one right next to the airport. Something that seems too convenient is probably tacky and should be avoided, and breaking these rules will set off an internal gay alarm.

BASIC NEEDS FOR HUMAN SURVIVAL

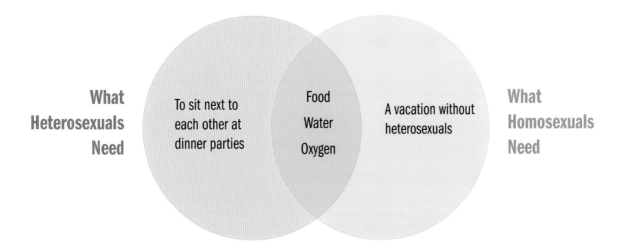

What Heterosexuals Need

To sit next to each other at dinner parties

Food
Water
Oxygen

A vacation without heterosexuals

What Homosexuals Need

The Ferry and Flight Response

The Ferry and Flight Response is a **homo-physiological** reaction that occurs when planning a trip. If getting to a vacation destination requires fewer than two separate modes of transportation, the homosexual body will enter a complete state of shock and refuse to book a trip to this spot. If a homosexual declines your suggestion of a vacation destination, this might be the Ferry and Flight Response at work. Try increasing the travel inconvenience level before asking them again!

A homosexual on his eighteenth consecutive hour of travel so he can take drugs on an island with strangers.

Gay Isolation

Because queer people are all about inclusion or whatever, they can't outright exclude heterosexuals from their spaces. To circumnavigate this issue, gays make things more difficult for themselves so that straight people won't follow suit.

Gays aren't excluding heterosexuals; they are achieving their desired outcome by letting heterosexuals make their own choices to exclude themselves. This is how **gay isolation** works. When it comes to planning a vacation, removing accessibility is the key to avoiding straight families from the suburbs and their loud children. This is why gay vacation spots need at least two different modes of transportation.

Removing Heterosexuals from Gaycation Spaces

A straight person at a gay destination can put a homosexual's mental and physical health at risk. As a safety precaution, gays will make every element of their vacation experience extremely inconvenient. This ensures that a heterosexual who stumbles upon it would never want to return, or worse, tell their hetero friends they should come here too.

This is why many gay parties are hosted at obscure locations you can get to but can't ever get home from. It's also by design that gay vacation spots lack cell service or dependable Wi-Fi. And it's no accident that you need to book your rental house eight years in advance. The taxis in Tulum and Mykonos are expensive and unavailable for a good reason! All these barriers have been carefully crafted by gay men. Gays are willing to deal with these inconveniences themselves in order to preserve their own health.

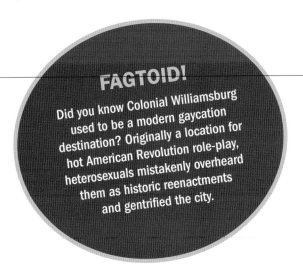

FAGTOID!

Did you know Colonial Williamsburg used to be a modern gaycation destination? Originally a location for hot American Revolution role-play, heterosexuals mistakenly overheard them as historic reenactments and gentrified the city.

Isolation Adrenaline

Have you ever seen how tightly bats fit together inside a cave? Or how bees swarm all over one another? Or how people trample retail workers on Black Friday? These animals borrow this kind of smothering behavior from homosexuals. The gay desire to be around the greatest number of gays with the least amount of personal space provides a natural high. As they pack themselves into an isolated place that lacks proper resources, adrenaline kicks in. What if something bad happens? They are all one emergency away from certain death, and there's nothing more exciting than that!

Dehydrated gay men partying 300 miles away from the nearest hospital.

The inside of an active volcano, the official host for World Pride 2043.

Some gay men enjoy getting high and then surrounding themselves with multiple ways to drown.

Serving Conclusions

→ Gay men love making things difficult for themselves.

→ Gay men put themselves in danger for fun, and that's okay!

→ Mykonos doesn't have any cabs.

Doppelbängers

The Tea: They really took "Go fuck yourself" literally.

Get PrEPared

You'll learn how to:

✔ **Recall** six popular theories behind doppelbängers

✔ **Identify** doppelbänger warning signs

Why it's important:

✔ Understanding your doppelbänger friends better will help you make funnier jokes at their expense.

A Case of Twincest

Why do some people in lesbian and gay relationships look so similar to their partners? With matching hairstyles, facial features, and fashion senses, it often feels like they could be twins! Gay Science calls these doppelbängers: gay couples who look identical to one another. There are a few theories as to why this scientific phenomenon is specific to queer couples:

Rejection Theory

Are these people just attracted to themselves? Initially thought to be a case of implicit egotism, researchers have found the opposite may be true. Queer men and women have such a strong fear of rejection, they may settle for someone who looks exactly like them. Because how can you reject someone who looks exactly like you?

Some questions to think about here: How would you rank your looks on a scale from 1–10? How does your partner rank? When you pursue someone who looks like you, does it even matter?

A male doppelbänger couple.

A female doppelbänger couple.

Comparison Theory

Similar to the rejection theory, some gays and lesbians avoid being compared to their partner by dating someone identical to them. This choice may backfire if one partner is more likable, leading to the other one being labeled as "off-brand" or a "knockoff."

Parental Theory

Calling all daddy and mommy issues! If there's a significant height or age difference in a doppelbänger couple, a familial connection might be at play.

Race Theory

Some people may find all others outside of their race similar-looking. This is something they should work on privately. The gay scientific community does not recommend calling couples outside of your race doppelbängers, except white people, who are always fair game.

The Clone Theory

Because gay dating has been made increasingly difficult due to a reduced dating pool (see our chapter on demography), some gay people have chosen to grow their partner in a lab. Because it is universally illegal to use another person's DNA without their permission, gays have been forced to use their own.

The Southern State Theory

Some gay couples look like siblings because they actually are.

Are You in a Doppelbänger?

Here are some warning signs:

- People call you by your partner's name.
- People call your partner by your name.
- You can't tell yourselves apart in a photo.
- You're at least a 50 percent match in a DNA test.

FAGTOID!

Calling two people outside your race "twins" is a good way to get canceled.

Serving Conclusions

→ Insecurity drives all gay choices, probably.

→ You can't clone people without their permission.

→ If you're south of the Mason–Dixon Line, that gay couple might actually be brothers.

Why Do Same-Sex Parents Raise Happier Kids?

The Tea: The lucky ones get two moms or dads.

Same-Sex Parents

Why have Christian conservatives been battling against same-sex couples becoming parents? Do you think they're aware that gay parents tend to raise the bar way higher when it comes to parenting compared to their straight counterparts?

Intention

Most human bodies are hardwired to want sex, and a lot of it. It's one of the easiest activities two people can participate in together. While asexual people live a blissful life without it (and we have a chapter on that), other humans have to deal with the accidental consequences of this natural desire: the creation of an entire human being.

They were just horny, and now they have this thing forever.

However, most gay couples can't be parents without the *intention* of becoming parents. Gay people are often satisfied with the progress of their personal goals before making this decision, so they don't place their unattained ambitions upon their children like straight people do, pressuring them to live the lives they wish they had before they got pregnant.

"You're gonna be all the things Mommy wanted to be until she had you!"

Financial Stability

Gay parents have to go through expensive and tedious processes to have a child through donors, adoption, or surrogacy. Raising kids costs a lot of money, so these barriers prequalify them as parents who can financially support their kids.

Perspective

Queer people are often born into straight households that don't understand them, but eventually they are able to experience the joy of being able to live as they are. This joy is ingrained in every piece of a queer person's parenting, from gender expression to hobbies and activities. Kids raised by gay parents are less likely to live with the pressure to be someone they aren't.

If we had to guess why Christian conservatives have battled against same-sex parenting for decades, we'd probably tell you it's because they know it's better. This widespread knowledge might expose their own bad parenting that has led to childhood abuse and broken foster care systems. But we're just a *Gay Science* textbook. What do we know?

OR (true) (false)

Same-sex parents will make their child gay.

Only the chosen ones are gay, and same-sex parents can't control this.

Opposite-sex parents will make their child straight.

Once again, only the chosen ones are gay.

Married parents can make their child single forever.

After children experience what marriage looks like, some will never, ever want something like that.

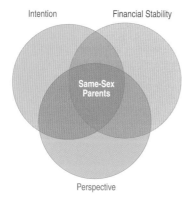

Intention — Financial Stability — Same-Sex Parents — Perspective

Serving Conclusions

→ Gay couples can't get pregnant by mistake.

→ Kids are insanely expensive.

→ Christian conservatives need to focus on their own kids.

Why Do Gay Guys Write Like Girls?

The Tea: That's the gayest penmanship I've ever seen.

Get PrEPared

You'll learn how to:

✔ **Identify** a gay just by looking at his writing assignment

✔ **Understand** what social constructs are

Why it's important:

✔ Owning your femme is the first step in understanding why you're better.

Be Sure to Heart Your i's

We know female teachers prefer their gay male students, but what about students who don't show the typical behaviors of a homosexual? How will the teacher choose her yearlong student bestie if he isn't showing the easy signs? Gay Science tells us that there are infinite ways to identify a gay, whether it's their voice, their run, or their music. Handwriting has always been one of them! Let's imagine that two boys are asked to complete a creative writing assignment. Do you think you would be able to distinguish the homosexual from the heterosexual? Compare the work of two different boys in in the chart below:

HOW TO IDENTIFY A GAY FROM A CREATIVE WRITING ASSIGNMENT

	Gay	Not Gay
Characters	Most characters will have first and last names and full, rich, dramatic backstories that aren't essential to the story whatsoever. At least one character has a secret power.	Fanfiction that features a famous athlete as the protagonist. At least one of their characters is their own dad.
Supplemental Materials	The front of the black three-ring laminated binder has a full-color illustrated cover. There will be addendums with family trees of the characters, visual aids, and a map. You can scan a QR code that directs you to a blog where the student will post future installments of the story.	One staple.
Handwriting	Super femme.	Was this written on a bus as it was hitting dozens of potholes?

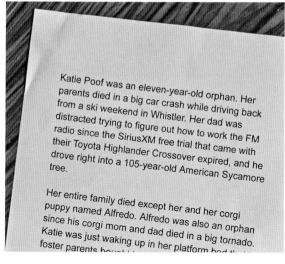

Katie Poof was an eleven-year-old orphan. Her parents died in a big car crash while driving back from a ski weekend in Whistler. Her dad was distracted trying to figure out how to work the FM radio since the SiriusXM free trial that came with their Toyota Highlander Crossover expired, and he drove right into a 105-year-old American Sycamore tree.

Her entire family died except her and her corgi puppy named Alfredo. Alfredo was also an orphan since his corgi mom and dad died in a big tornado. Katie was just waking up in her platform bed th... foster parents bough...

A gay boy will bring fully fleshed out characters—and lots of drama.

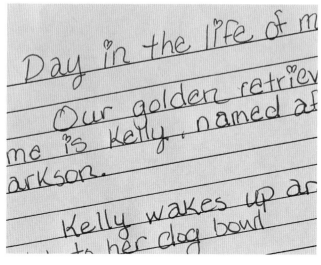

Day in the life of m...
Our golden retriev...
me is Kelly, named af...
arkson.

Kelly wakes up an...
... to her dog bowl...

Gay handwriting. Notice the letter A.

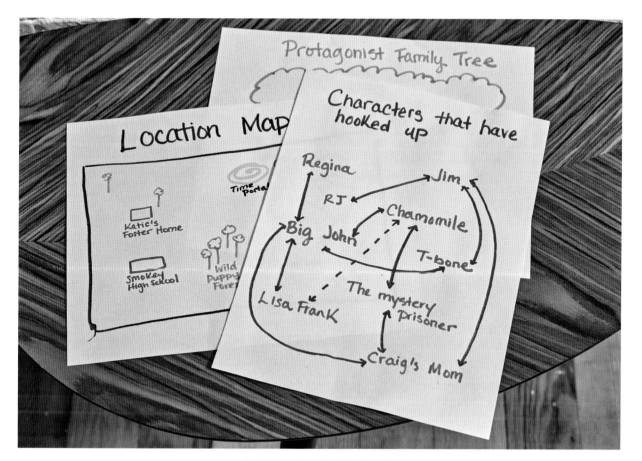

Homosexual supplemental material.

Graphology

Graphology is the science behind handwriting, which uses strokes and symmetry to determine how evil a person is. The larger scientific community has rejected this study as pseudoscience, though France considers it legitimate and still uses it today. Because France is super, super, super gay, we also consider it to be real science!

What Is Girly Handwriting?

The idea of feminine handwriting is a contemporary social construct, because only about a century ago, this kind of writing was known simply as *legible penmanship*. It wasn't such a novel concept for a man to have neat, orderly, premium writing. So why are women and gay men the only ones who write like this now? Let's look at social constructs to try to understand.

Social Constructs Around You

Social norms are the rules of conduct that make people more boring by dictating how they should behave. We'll explain which of the following topics are social constructs:

Yas! OR **NAUR**
(true) (false)

Status symbols

Yas!

Expensive cars and designer jockstraps.

The attractiveness of your height

Yas!

Why does 6'0" look better than 5'11"?

Your literal height

NAUR

But you're really 5'10" though, and that's a fact, babe.

Intelligence

Yas!

Getting good grades at Harvard doesn't mean you can navigate a maximum security prison.

Backward Evolution

A kind of reversed evolution has come about due to the decline in the standards of the modern heterosexual male. This group of men are currently going through the early stages of a mass backward evolution (or de-evolution). Historically, the fittest members of a species would procreate to pass down better attributes, but now the dumbest people procreate the most, and the smartest the least. This has caused a **cismutation** to occur in the straight man as they regress into a more primitive form.

As straight men started to devolve, gays were forced to mask their handwriting as terrible or else be publicly humiliated. Though some of them actually enjoyed this!

These new, less-advanced men have found other ways to normalize their inferior traits by ostracizing those who haven't devolved yet. All sorts of things were shunned as effeminate in real newspaper articles:

- Having initials on a bathrobe (1925)
- Eating cooked meat (1940)
- Using toiletries (1965)
- Living in a high-rise apartment (1977)
- Passing out (1983)
- Using hair gel (2004)
- Listening to the *Titanic* soundtrack (2004)
- Drinking from juice boxes (2014)

This isn't the first time in history we've seen the genetically inferior dictate what's socially acceptable, but girly handwriting is finally making its comeback.

The *Titanic* Soundtrack and Hair Gel in 2004

"There's even a new name for this category of guy—metrosexual. He's a man who's not afraid of Celine Dion or a little hair gel."

—Mary Ethridge, *Daily Herald*

Juice Boxes in 2014

"After you're done drinking your little juice boxes . . . you're ready to put makeup on. You're ready to wear a short skirt."

—Alex Jones, Human Toilet

Inbred royals who couldn't physically close their mouths used to decide what was acceptable in society.

Serving Conclusions

→ Gay kids love character development.
→ You know a gay letter A when you see it.
→ Juice boxes have no gender.

Game-Night Lesbians, Explained

The Tea: The dykes are staying in tonight.

A Fascinating Subtype

Within the lesbian nomenclature there is a subtype of **game-night lesbians**: gay women who fucking love a night of partying that involves playing board games.

They are either hosting weekly game nights or secretly hoping one breaks out. There are three primary lesbian qualities that contribute to this:

A lesbian hoping this turns into a game night ASAP.

Competitive

While queer men and straight women feel vulnerable talking about their skills and talents, straight men and queer women wear them like badges. Games are attractive to lesbians because there is a game for every skill combination, and they provide a way for lesbians to see how they stack up against others in 40 minutes or less.

You can really learn a lot about someone's skills after a round of **Taboo**:

Skills Tested:

- Pop Culture Knowledge
- Interpersonal Communication
- Time Management
- Reading Comprehension
- Memory
- Multitasking Skills
- Anger Management
- Adherence to the Rules
- Trustworthiness
- Ability to Deal with Deb

Want to Do Something, But Like, Not Too Much

A gay female is rarely satisfied doing absolutely nothing. However, when plans become ambitious they can start to feel complicated or exhausting. Isn't there a bowl of porridge that's just right? Game nights hit the sweet spot within the Lesbian Activity Window as a highly engaging activity that doesn't require them to leave the house.

LESBIAN ACTIVITY WINDOW

I'm bored, let's do something   Game night!   Oh, that sounds very involved . . .

Getting to Know Someone

A large social mixer with a bunch of strangers is a nightmare for a lesbian. When it comes to engaging in small talk, lesbians rank dead last.

They would rather get to know someone new in a living room with a game that shows them who they really are. "Sure, you work in advertising and have two younger siblings, but can you score a Quiplash?"

Game	Action	What this says to a lesbian
Codenames	4 cards with 1 word	They have a good relationship with their partner
Murder Mystery	Making a baseless accusation	They're erratic and wild and I find that hot
Scattergories	Using an adjective in front of the word to steal points	They need to leave my home immediately

LIKELIHOOD OF SMALL TALK

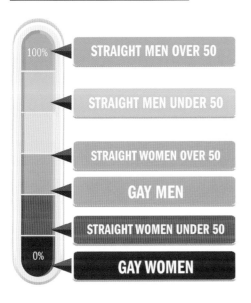

100%

STRAIGHT MEN OVER 50

STRAIGHT MEN UNDER 50

STRAIGHT WOMEN OVER 50

GAY MEN

STRAIGHT WOMEN UNDER 50

0%

GAY WOMEN

A LESBIAN KICKING OUT A SCATTERGORIES CHEATER:

"You just put 'super' in front of every word? Sorry, you have to leave."

Serving Conclusions

→ Lesbians love their living rooms.

→ Lesbians cut right to the chase.

→ Cheating in Scattergories is unforgivable.

Horror-Genre Gays, Explained

The Tea: Why is Jason Voorhees so hot?

Get PrEPared

You'll learn how to:

✔ **Identify** the three reasons why horror gays exist

✔ **Understand** where your anonymous kink comes from

Why it's important:

✔ Halloween has always been gay.

Jessica Biel runs through the meat racks in *The Texas Chainsaw Massacre*.

A homosexual runs through the meat racks on Fire Island.

A Spooky Subtype

From Buffy to Dragula, to Ryan Murphy, gay people are singlehandedly keeping the horror entertainment industry afloat. This is thanks to the horror-genre gay. We'll discuss the three main reasons why this type of homosexual is obsessed with all things spooky.

Theatrics

Gay men thrive on drama. The combination of camp and death proves to be an irresistible combination for many of them. A landline phone ringing in a massive house in the suburbs gives them purpose. A group of teenagers stranded in an inbred small town makes them feel alive—especially when it includes the thrill of Jessica Biel running through the meat racks. Something gay men know quite well.

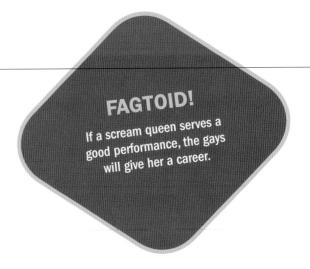

FAGTOID!

If a scream queen serves a good performance, the gays will give her a career.

Feminine Power

Horror films often choose a strong female lead, which gay men are drawn to.

A woman rising to power or surviving the unthinkable fuels a homosexual. It is powerful feminine energy. Gay men like to see themselves as similar to this kind of main character: brave, resourceful, born with a special gift, and not being afraid to use it.

Cunty Female Horror Leads

- Sidney in *Scream*
- Julie James in *I Know What You Did Last Summer*
- Laurie Strode in *Halloween*
- Ellen Ripley in *Alien*
- Dani in *Midsommar*
- Cindy and Brenda in *Scary Movie*
- Rachel Keller in *The Ring*
- Melania Trump in her own life

Anon Villains

Many gay men find something erotic in a concealed identity. Which is why these "DL" villains are such an attractive class.

Gay men are mostly interested in someone when they know absolutely nothing about them and progressively lose interest in that person the more they learn who they really are. If a gay man was in a horror movie he would be lining up to meet the masked murderer.

Toxic men with an unknown identity, terrible conversation skills, and practically no personality prove irresistible to the homosexual.

A GAY:

"Don't take off the mask when you murder me. It will ruin it."

Daddy.

Serving Conclusions

→ A female badass is everything.

→ No really, though, Jason Voorhees could get it.

What Does It Mean to Be Intersex?

The Tea: Let's leave the baby's genitals alone, please!

A husband and wife celebrating that their kid will have a penis.

Fucking Up Your Gender Reveal

Procreators are one of the most fascinating creatures on our planet. They focus on the strangest things! While child-free people could literally care less about the sex of children, those who procreate are obsessed with the subject. Procreators will throw color-coded **gender reveal parties** to announce a tiny baby penis (blue) or a vagina (pink) and then set a forest on fire in celebration. Not only do these procreators not know the difference between sex and gender (they're having a sex party for babies—just callin' it like it is), but they are also setting themselves up for trouble when their baby's sex announcement should have exploded in the color purple. These are **intersex** babies: making people upset about their existence before they are even born.

Structure and Gay-gency

Intersex people are born with a combination of male and female traits, like testicles (male) and a uterus (female), or a penis (male) and being paid less for doing the same amount of work (female). In sociology, there are two different ways intersex people can exist in their own bodies: **structure** and **gay-gency**.

Structure

Some rules within our social world exist to make everyone more comfortable. It's why it's rude to stare at a stranger for a very long time with a gun in your hand. But others exist to make one person who sticks out feel worse about themselves. Why does someone say "Bless you" when another person sneezes? Shaming the sneezer (who everyone heard, by the way) under the guise of a small prayer? We're not buying it, Sandra.

Because procreators are obsessed with what kids have down there, they've created a social norm to make it perfectly acceptable to change someone's sex without their knowledge or consent. Many intersex people never even got the chance to live as they were born, or decide their own sex. And it's not just the parents signing off on newborn sex changes. Doctors will hold up babies right after they are delivered, take a look at the flaps, then decide what to snip without even asking the parents. (This is literally true.)

Gay-gency

Queer social agency, also known as gay-gency, allows the intersex person to have full control over their choices. This means they have the freedom to live as they were born, the freedom to remove or not remove anything on their own body, and the freedom to order delivery even though there's meal prep in the fridge.

Social Norms   **Felonies**

Respecting personal boundaries

Paying attention to personal hygiene

Chopping someone's dick off without their permission

Silencing your phone during a performance

Waiting in line patiently

Setting a house on fire

Misappropriating funds

Robbing a person at gunpoint

Being a terrorist

Stealing someone's identity

Human Bodies Are Weird, Babe

If you think it's strange that nature gave someone both breasts and a penis, have you thought about how weird those things are on their own? Breasts are mostly useless fat sacs that churn out a few rounds of cloudy water, while a penis is a dangly skin tag that becomes a blood balloon when it sees a pair of fat sacs, then produces cloudy water of its own. Everything your body does is cringe, but that's your own business.

FAGTOID!

Politically conservative and religious people who don't believe trans kids (or adults, let's be real) should have gender-affirming care would drool at the chance to give their own intersex newborn a sex change!

Serving Conclusions

→ It's weird enough just writing about baby penises, let alone knowing some people throw parties for them!

→ Something illegal can become socially acceptable once it targets the LGBTQ+.

→ All bodies are embarrassing.

Are Pansexual People Living Better Lives?

The Tea: Why be a love seat when you can be modular furniture?

The Pansexuals Have Arrived

Most letters under the LGBTQ+ Pavilion do not experience the wide dating pool that heterosexuals enjoy, though one letter has smartly gamed the system to find their ultimate best life. These are **pansexuals**: human efficiency machines who do not limit their sexual or romantic attraction to individuals based on gender.

Like solar energy, pansexual people are highly efficient machines with unlimited renewable resources.

Is It Laissez-Faire?

You might imagine pansexuals as carefree and easygoing, but this is the work of their fantastic PR team. They are a highly analytical and methodical group who have calculated their optimal situation using a variety of techniques and practices. They are the Dwight Schrutes of the LGBTQ+.

Qualitative vs. Quantitative Romance

Most queer people start with the qualities they desire in a partner then gradually narrow down their search until they find the best one. This is known as **qualitative dating**, and it's why so many of them are still single (and will be forever).

Pansexual people utilize **quantitative dating**, where literally no person is off the table for any reason. Regardless of gender or criminal record, a person isn't going to be scrapped for arbitrary things before there's a chance to meet. But being pansexual doesn't mean they don't have preferences.

Most pansexuals are likely to score as the EHKP type in the Admires-Wiggs Personality Indicator test. You can find out your personality type in the experiment at the end of this chapter!

Things with Pansexual Energy

A universal remote.

A Swiss Army Knife.

A true vers.

Social Exchange Theory

Claude Levi-Denim was a pansexual ethnologist who lived to be 100 years old by getting constant emotionally rich sexual experiences with quality partners for eighty decades. Levi-Denim was having "I love you" sex up until his last breath. He did this by combining quantitative dating with pansexual cost-benefit analysis.

PANSEXUAL COST-BENEFIT ANALYSIS

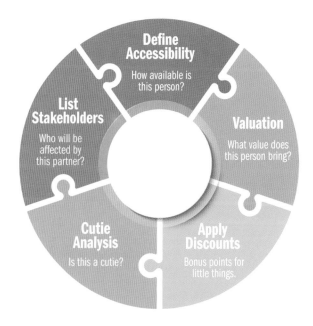

Define Accessibility
How available is this person?

Valuation
What value does this person bring?

Apply Discounts
Bonus points for little things.

Cutie Analysis
Is this a cutie?

List Stakeholders
Who will be affected by this partner?

Serving Conclusions

→ Pansexual people are living better lives.

→ If you can't keep up with these systems, consider bisexuality.

→ I am not actually a true vers.

ACTIVITY

What Admires-Wiggs Personality Type Are You?

The queer cousin of Myers-Briggs, Admires-Wiggs is a personality type indicator to determine what kind of queer you are. With this brief examination, you'll self-report your own score in four parts to learn which one of the 16 different personalities you fall under.

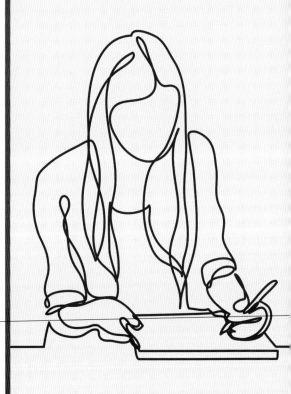

HOW TO TAKE THE TEST

You'll be presented with different statements. Answer with a number (1–7) based on how much you agree or disagree with that statement:

1 - Strongly agree
2 - Agree
3 - Somewhat agree
4 - Neither agree nor disagree
5 - Somewhat disagree
6 - Disagree
7 - Strongly disagree

You'll tally up your score for each section and assign yourself a letter. At the end of all four parts you'll discover your full 4-letter type. If you don't think that fits your personality, then you're probably just straight.

PART 1

My conversations feel like performances.

☐ 1 ☐ 2 ☐ 3 ☐ 4 ☐ 5 ☐ 6 ☐ 7

I wouldn't be seen dead in a strip mall.

☐ 1 ☐ 2 ☐ 3 ☐ 4 ☐ 5 ☐ 6 ☐ 7

I won't leave the house without looking cute even if I'm just running a quick errand.

☐ 1 ☐ 2 ☐ 3 ☐ 4 ☐ 5 ☐ 6 ☐ 7

Everything in my life is customized.

☐ 1 ☐ 2 ☐ 3 ☐ 4 ☐ 5 ☐ 6 ☐ 7

I hate circuit music.

☐ 1 ☐ 2 ☐ 3 ☐ 4 ☐ 5 ☐ 6 ☐ 7

I never use drag queen lingo in my everyday conversations.

☐ 1 ☐ 2 ☐ 3 ☐ 4 ☐ 5 ☐ 6 ☐ 7

Top 40 pop music is my personal hell.

☐ 1 ☐ 2 ☐ 3 ☐ 4 ☐ 5 ☐ 6 ☐ 7

TOTAL SCORE:
7–29 = Extra [E]
>29 = Basic [B]

PART 2

I love sex.

☐ 1 ☐ 2 ☐ 3 ☐ 4 ☐ 5 ☐ 6 ☐ 7

I think a strip club is fun.

☐ 1 ☐ 2 ☐ 3 ☐ 4 ☐ 5 ☐ 6 ☐ 7

Poppers are for the bedroom and not the dance floor.

☐ 1 ☐ 2 ☐ 3 ☐ 4 ☐ 5 ☐ 6 ☐ 7

I am turned on by cartoon characters.

☐ 1 ☐ 2 ☐ 3 ☐ 4 ☐ 5 ☐ 6 ☐ 7

I am turned on by my trauma.

☐ 1 ☐ 2 ☐ 3 ☐ 4 ☐ 5 ☐ 6 ☐ 7

The Grinch could get it.

☐ 1 ☐ 2 ☐ 3 ☐ 4 ☐ 5 ☐ 6 ☐ 7

I'm having sex right now.

☐ 1 ☐ 2 ☐ 3 ☐ 4 ☐ 5 ☐ 6 ☐ 7

TOTAL SCORE:
7–33 = Horny [H]
>33 = Not Horny [N]

PART 3

I haven't left my bed all day
and that's probably not good.

☐ 1 ☐ 2 ☐ 3 ☐ 4 ☐ 5 ☐ 6 ☐ 7

I don't have healthy habits.

☐ 1 ☐ 2 ☐ 3 ☐ 4 ☐ 5 ☐ 6 ☐ 7

I know when I'm being
irrational, but I still do it anyway.

☐ 1 ☐ 2 ☐ 3 ☐ 4 ☐ 5 ☐ 6 ☐ 7

If you put me in charge of
something, you might regret it.

☐ 1 ☐ 2 ☐ 3 ☐ 4 ☐ 5 ☐ 6 ☐ 7

I like to see how much I can get away
with before I hit rock bottom.

☐ 1 ☐ 2 ☐ 3 ☐ 4 ☐ 5 ☐ 6 ☐ 7

I joke about my own issues.

☐ 1 ☐ 2 ☐ 3 ☐ 4 ☐ 5 ☐ 6 ☐ 7

I am in my flop era.

☐ 1 ☐ 2 ☐ 3 ☐ 4 ☐ 5 ☐ 6 ☐ 7

TOTAL SCORE:
7–29 = Mentally unwell and you know it [K]
>29 = Mentally unwell and you don't know it [D]

PART 4

I'd rather be on a date than
at a friend's birthday dinner.

☐ 1 ☐ 2 ☐ 3 ☐ 4 ☐ 5 ☐ 6 ☐ 7

The purpose of attending a party
is to go home with someone.

☐ 1 ☐ 2 ☐ 3 ☐ 4 ☐ 5 ☐ 6 ☐ 7

I'm not a big fan of group chats.

☐ 1 ☐ 2 ☐ 3 ☐ 4 ☐ 5 ☐ 6 ☐ 7

Being single is a lonely experience.

☐ 1 ☐ 2 ☐ 3 ☐ 4 ☐ 5 ☐ 6 ☐ 7

I don't mind competing against my
friends if we both like the same person.

☐ 1 ☐ 2 ☐ 3 ☐ 4 ☐ 5 ☐ 6 ☐ 7

The best part about finding a romantic
partner is not having to go out as much.

☐ 1 ☐ 2 ☐ 3 ☐ 4 ☐ 5 ☐ 6 ☐ 7

If I'm attracted to my friend's ex,
I will probably get with them.

☐ 1 ☐ 2 ☐ 3 ☐ 4 ☐ 5 ☐ 6 ☐ 7

TOTAL SCORE:
7–29 = Partner-focused [P]
>29 = Friend-focused [F]

Find your personality type!

MIRANDAS

The most well-rounded and likable class of queer.

ENKF: Will always pick a house party over a circuit party. Will settle for a game night.

BNKF: The most trustworthy of all queer personality types. They'll put a bestie before anyone else.

ENDF: They have a high standard for friendship, but once they trust you, you're in. Very good at spotting red flags.

BNDF: You may keep forgetting who this person is even though you met them multiple times, but once it finally clicks, they make for a great friend.

CHARLOTTES

The conservative, cautious queers.

ENKP: They keep a list of all the fun, exciting things they want to do with their partner. Now they just need to get one.

BNKP: Have literally the worst luck but keep a good sense of humor.

ENDP: They finally got accepted into Raya and won't shut up about it.

BNDP: Some people would call them boring, but they'd call themselves consistent.

SAMANTHAS

The horniest ones we know and we absolutely love them for it.

EHKF: Early adopter. Introduces their friends to cool things before everyone else catches on. Knows where the hot people are.

BHKF: The greatest energy. Absolute goddamn chaos.

EHDF: They don't chase people, they attract.

BHDF: So very unbothered by the judgment of others. They wake up every day feeling blessed they aren't straight.

CARRIES

They are the center of their universe and nothing will get in their way.

EHKP: If they wanted to, they could make your life an absolute nightmare.

BHKP: The horniest of all sixteen types and they'd be the first ones to admit it. Spend every waking moment flipping between dating apps.

EHDP: Charming, exciting, driven. Have excellent taste in potential partners and won't settle for someone mediocre. And they'll never need to.

BHDP: Would sell their best friend down the river for some good sex.

The Gay Social Order

The Tea: Are you a noble or a peasant?

Get PrEPared

You'll learn how to:

✔ **Identify** the gays who think they're on top

✔ **Identify** the gays who are actually on top

✔ **Understand** that they're all bottoms

Why it's important:

✔ If you want to dismantle the system, then you're probably at the bottom.

The Gay Pecking Order

Not all homosexuals are created equal. Some have followers and brand deals!

While some have influence, some have money, and others have over eight inches, what you bring to the table can determine your value in the community. The upper class gets first dibs when it comes to access, opportunities, and sex. Here's how the gay social classes sort themselves out.

The Noble Divas

Dolly, Mariah, Whitney. The highest echelon of existence. They are above the concept of a sexuality.

Gay Nobility

EGOT winners, mid-level female pop singers, any celebrity named Jennifer.

The Clergy

Gays who own one house in the city and then another by a body of water, excluding the Ozarks.

The Bourgeoisie

Obnoxious party promoters who are painful but necessary connections, Internet-famous people, your drug dealer, gays who own one house in the city and then another by a body of water, if it's in the Ozarks.

The Peasants

Gays who don't bring their own drugs to parties, but they keep showing up because they got an invite somehow.

The Serfs

Suburban gays on Grindr when you're visiting home, Log Cabin Republicans (hung).

The Outlaws

The overserved five-foot-nothing at the bar who won't leave you alone, Log Cabin Republicans (not hung).

Dress Codes

Historically, for heterosexuals, social order and class dictated fashion and appropriate dress. This does not apply to queer people, who have a more liberal view of their wardrobe. Dress codes do not exist. You'll never be able to tell where friends are going from their outfits alone. A group of gay friends can attend the same function and all dress completely different.

GAY PECKING ORDER

THE NOBLE DIVAS

GAY NOBILITY

THE CLERGY

THE BOURGEOISIE

THE PEASANTS

THE SERFS

THE OUTLAWS

A GAY MAN IN ATHLEISURE:

"I don't jog. I'm just dressed like I do."

Serving Conclusions

→ Jennifer celebrities are gay icons.

→ We're not going to the Ozarks.

→ Sportswear on a gay? Chic. Sportswear on a straight? Basic.

The Big Gay Economy

The Tea: You're not broke, it's just science.

Get PrEPared

You'll learn how to:

✔ **Identify** what gay men spend their money on
✔ **Understand** what FOMO is
✔ **Explain** Gayme Theory

Why it's important:

✔ Where are gays getting all this money from?

Homo Economics

According to neoclassic economic theory, **homo economicus** are "individuals who exhibit rationality and a narrow focus on their own self-interest while pursuing their personally defined objectives in an optimal manner." Okay, enough of that.

In other words, they think about themselves all the time, and use logic to achieve their goals. This is how homosexuals look at a lot of things in life, with finances being one of them.

So gays have money, sure. But where does all the gay money go? And where do they get their funds when it seems like they never work? How have they been on a dozen trips already and it's not even April? The director of finance and credit card points at the **Monét X Change Academy** found what gay people spend their money on.

What Do Gay Men Spend Their Money On?

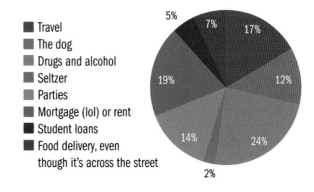

■ Travel
■ The dog
■ Drugs and alcohol
■ Seltzer
■ Parties
■ Mortgage (lol) or rent
■ Student loans
■ Food delivery, even though it's across the street

But inside the gay bubble, there's a secondary partying economy with rules of its own.

Gay Production

A gay party needs three things:

• **Drugs and alcohol**
• **Gays**
• **Music**

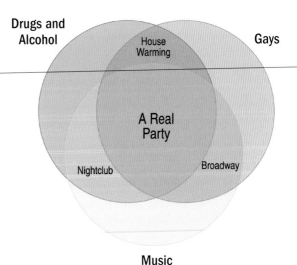

Opportunity Cost

FOMO, or fear of missed orgies, drives all homosexual choices. Missing out on the big event, DJ set, or sex party will send them into deep depression. The gay will spiral thinking about what kind of connections and k-holes he missed out on. If a gay man misses three big parties in a row, he becomes invisible to the community and must work twice as hard to find out when the next ones will be.

The cost of missing out on a social event often outweighs the cost of the ticket. Gay men will buy two or three pairs of passes to multiple events throughout the year without knowing any of the details. They'll buy several tickets for competing Pride events just to have the option to go where the crowd goes, which isn't clear until a few hours before. The stress of acquiring a sold-out ticket ages gay men significantly, so they choose to grab a bunch of them first and worry about which event they'll actually go to later.

Supply and Demand

Because gay men would rather attend a party than plan for a financial future, the cost of gay parties have skyrocketed due to **price determination**.

Gayme Theory

Gayme theory helps gay men determine the best plan for the weekend by guessing what social opportunities they will enjoy based on their actions and the actions of others.

Top/Bottom Theory

Let's look at the potential outcomes of whether tops and bottoms decide to stay in or go out.

If all the tops and bottoms decide to go out tonight, there will be sexual equity at the club. If only one group decides to stay in while the other goes out, there will be an oversaturation of that type at the party. But if they both stay in, they can find compatible people on the apps

		TOPS	
		Goes Out	**Stays In**
BOTTOMS	**Goes Out**	Sexual equity at the party	All bottoms at the party
	Stays In	All tops at the party	Meet on the apps

After-Hours Theory

When trying to conserve your energy and money, going to all the parties available that night might be impossible. Pregaming during the main event and then hitting the after-parties is a smart choice so you can hang out with the people you enjoy and then skip to the good stuff, if everyone else is also following this plan.

FAGTOID!

Gay torture: a gay man can handle waterboarding but they can't handle another party being more fun elsewhere.

	Hot people only go to the main party	Hot people only go to the afters
You go to the main party first	Perfect timing	You're wiped but at least the hotties are here now
You only go to the afters	An absolute disaster	You timed this perfectly *and* saved money

The hottest guy at the afters.

A MAN WHO MISSED THE ORGY:

"I have FOMO."

Serving Conclusions

- → **A gay dog is a spoiled dog.**
- → **This gay event is expensive as fuck.**
- → **There are never too many tops at a party. Let's be real.**

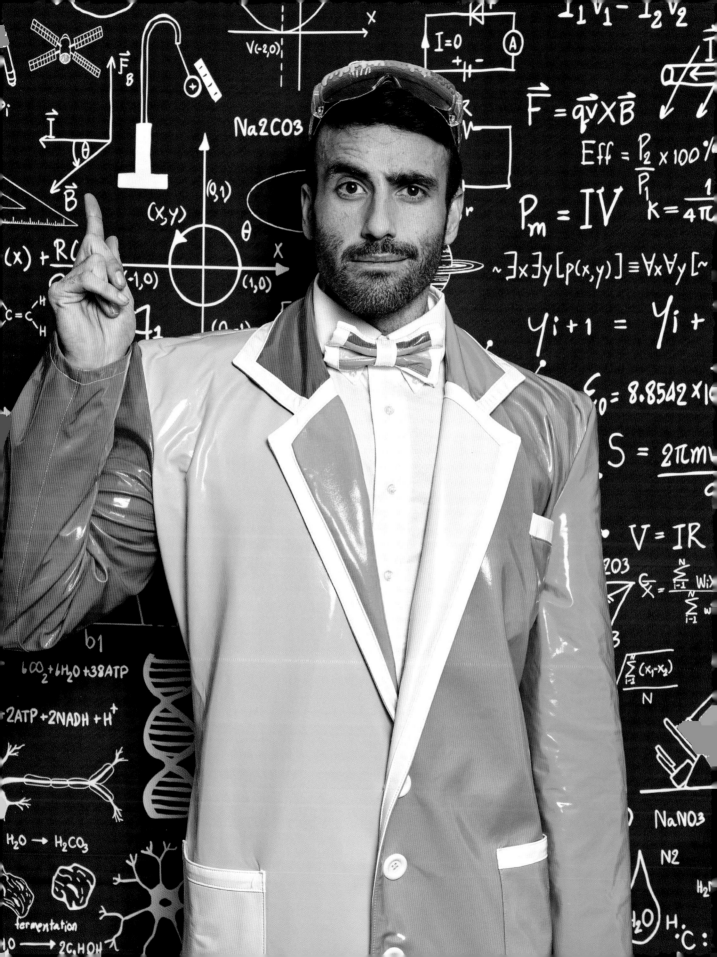

LGBTQ+ Crime and Punishment

The Tea: Shame! Shame!

Get PrEPared

You'll learn how to:

✔ **Identify** the two queer punishments

✔ **Compare and contrast** queer crimes

Why it's important:

✔ Some LGBTQ+ crimes are just too serious to ignore.

A white gay man shaming a stranger on Instagram for being at a party with too many white people there.

LGBTQ+ Punishment

For LGBTQ+ there's the punishment you like and the punishment you don't. We're not gonna get into the first kind, you pervert, but we would like to explore the two retaliatory measures the community takes against its own when that person behaves poorly.

Shame

Contrary to what most people may think, many queer people don't want a world without shame. Because shame is what many of them have only ever known, they'll always seek a way to have it around. The LGBTQ+ Pergola aggressively resists being stigmatized from outside sources so they can double down on shaming each other within. When a queer person has been shamed, this is known as wearing the **scarlet triangle**.

Queer people will expend more energy on shaming other LGBTQ+ people who don't post on social media about recent antigay legislation than they will on fighting the forces responsible for it. Not all queer-on-queer shame is so obvious, though. There's a lot you can be shamed for!

Exclusion

The worst queer punishment is being excluded. This is reserved for the most serious kinds of crimes. This can take the form of passive exclusion like ghosting or nonresponsiveness, or active exclusion, where the justice-seekers may tarnish the offender's reputation across the city. Some forms of active exclusion can be brutal, forcing the offender to leave the city altogether.

LGBTQ+ Crimes

Here is an inexhaustive list of the things that could incur a gay punishment, from least to most serious:

Fraud

A gay fraud shows their true colors with activities that go against the interests of their own community. For this crime, offenders will wear the scarlet triangle for a short period of time. Examples:

- Eating at Chick-fil-A
- Shopping at Hobby Lobby
- Voting conservative
- Misrepresenting themselves as vers

Sex Crimes

Depending on who has been affected, a sex crime could incur a laugh or a full-out active exclusion. Examples:

- Overstating one's height by at least two inches
- Suggesting condom use
- Saying you were ready to bottom but you were not ready to bottom
- Breaking up a power couple

Social Transgressions

Incurring a social condemnation will almost certainly lead to an exclusion punishment. Examples:

- Losing the group's baggie at the club
- Playing country music at the party
- Not posting about a recent topical social issue on Instagram

Embezzlement

Gay theft is the most serious of all crimes. Examples:

- Discovery theft
- Boyfriend theft

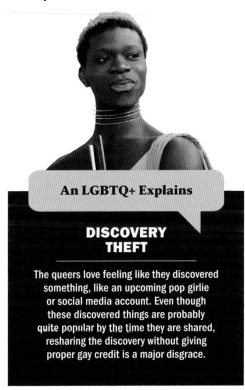

An LGBTQ+ Explains

DISCOVERY THEFT

The queers love feeling like they discovered something, like an upcoming pop girlie or social media account. Even though these discovered things are probably quite popular by the time they are shared, resharing the discovery without giving proper gay credit is a major disgrace.

Serving Conclusions

→ The horror of a condom!
→ Not the country music.
→ Where's my discovery credit?

PART 3

Formal Sciences

Traditional formal science systems like math, logic, and statistics are essential to innovation! They're also really, really boring. Formal Gay Science will read your fallacies to filth while wearing heels. It will postulate with good lower back posture. It cares about the proof of a statement *and* of the cocktail. And it knows that a function is both the relationship between inputs and outputs, and also the progressive house music thing they're gonna do drugs at tonight.

Forensics
Learn why gay people have such a hard time understanding math, and how it can help us understand throuples.

Engineering
Artificial intelligence and aromantic people have a lot of similarities. Are they one in the same?

Computer Science
Can computer systems and non-binary people coexist?

Logic
We use queer logic to answer your burning questions like why do queer people move so often, why are gay people always late, and are your children safe around the LGBTQ+?

Are Gay People Bad at Math?

The Tea: Numbers are so heteronormative.

Get PrEPared

You'll learn how to:

✔ **Identify** the seven gay gifts

✔ **Understand** who Alan Turing was

Why it's important:

✔ Making math gay is the first step to becoming better at it!

How Do You Solve a Problem?

Gay men aren't good tippers because they're generous. They just can't do math.

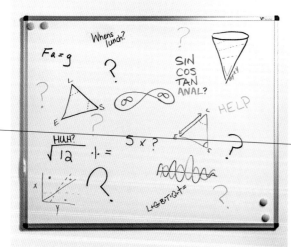

A gay man attempting math.

There are two main reasons why numbers just don't compute:

Math is Too Boring

Some homos *can* actually solve math problems, but they reject the notion based on how mundane it is. It's also incredibly accessible, a concept that gays refuse to recognize. *Everyone* has access to math, and homosexuals want no part in something so universal and mainstream. If most people in the world know about it and use it, then it's not good enough for the gays. Except public parks, which they seem to love after dark.

Math is Too Objective

Numbers are simple: they're either correct or they aren't. So where's the flavor? Where's the drama? Gay people avoid any objective systems where gayness provides no additional benefit. To them, objectivity is a death trap. Homosexuals prefer to manipulate a situation or solve problems using one of the other powers they are born with. These are the seven **gay gifts**.

THE SEVEN GAY GIFTS

Storytelling

Self-deprecation

Knowledge of pop culture

Going on vacation

Aesthetics

Observational humor

Being hung and/or tall

All gay men possess at least one of these gifts and rely on them to succeed or escape a bind. It's why so many gay men will boldly enter a club without any money whatsoever, or walk into a job interview with a completely fabricated resume. They'll make it work! None of these seven qualities are helpful when solving a math problem, so while some guys with multiple gay gifts could get away with murder, they still can't get away with PEDMAS.

The Daddy of Gay Math

Famous homosexual **Alan Turing** was born with the disease of understanding math, and was tortured by this affliction every day of his life. Determined to remove math entirely from our world, he operated under the guise of a pro-math mathematician and famously broke the Enigma code so the Germans couldn't use math anymore. He's a hero in the gay community for his passion to dismantle math systems.

Alan Turing, a gay man suffering from the illness of knowing math.

(true) OR (false)

Could an average gay man . . .

budget?

They're not gonna look at their own bank accounts, and they're certainly not going to do math with what they find.

use a coupon?

They don't know what 15 percent off is, and they're sure as hell not giving out their email for it.

learn a new currency?

Exchange rates? They'll never learn what theirs converts to.

Serving Conclusions

→ Gays are good at going on vacation.
→ Alan Turing was a king for putting up with all that math.
→ What does a peso convert to?

The Mathematics Behind a Throuple

The Tea: When LTR daddies get bored.

Get PrEPared

You'll learn how to:

✔ **Understand** how a throuple was invented

✔ **Compare and contrast** different types of throuple triangles

Why it's important:

✔ Throuple math is an essential skill.

Three blind mice: the first (and only) famous disabled homosexual throuple.

The First Threesome

On September 29, 2009, **Dr. Britney Spears** made a new discovery. The renowned geometric topologist broke through heteronormative systems to have the world's first ever threesome. We're paraphrasing here (because we legally have to), but it went something like this:

"One, two, three. There's someone else here besides you and me. Got one hundred and eighty degrees and I'm stuck between the two of you."

—Dr. Britney Spears, 2009

Unfortunately for Dr. Spears, that threesome was actually a vicious legal battle for her autonomy between her, her father, and the State of California. But her gift did not go unnoticed by the LGBTQ+ community, who then began having three-way relationships, or **throuples**.

A Matter of Triangles

Throuples may seem confusing, but they follow the rules of geometry! The three corners of the triangle represent the *people* inside the throuple, while the line between them (the walls) represent their *connection*.

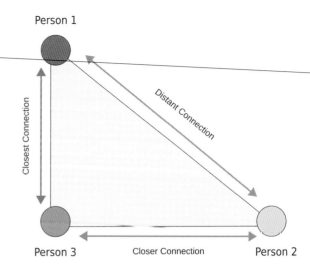

Throuples start as a line, with two dots connecting a couple that has been together for, like, 10 years. They evolve into a throuple when a third, younger, unemployed person enters the mix and moves into their nice home in Presidio Heights.

Triangle Inequality

A perfectly balanced triangle, or an **equi-dad-teral triangle**, has all equal sides. This is when the connections between all three members of the throuple are equally strong. Though ideal, a triangle of this type doesn't stay this way for long as other factors come into play that weaken the wall, like financial stress or being distracted by other, hotter lines and triangles. Here are a few of the throuple types you might see:

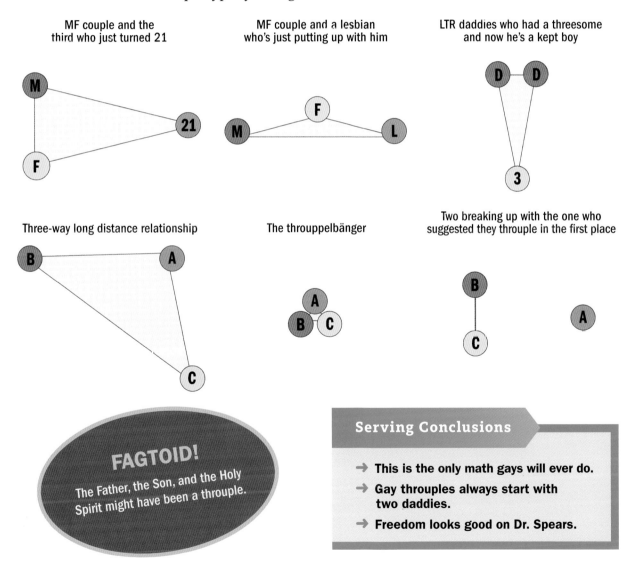

MF couple and the
third who just turned 21

MF couple and a lesbian
who's just putting up with him

LTR daddies who had a threesome
and now he's a kept boy

Three-way long distance relationship

The throuppelbänger

Two breaking up with the one who
suggested they throuple in the first place

FAGTOID!

The Father, the Son, and the Holy Spirit might have been a throuple.

Serving Conclusions

→ **This is the only math gays will ever do.**

→ **Gay throuples always start with two daddies.**

→ **Freedom looks good on Dr. Spears.**

Are Aromantic People Robots?

The Tea: Do aromantic people even have souls?

AN AROMANTIC AFTER LEARNING ABOUT ROMANTIC ATTRACTION:

"Those are the symptoms of a panic attack."

The New (A)Romantics

Aromantics experience very little romantic attraction, and sometimes none at all. For them, being friend-zoned is the goal. **Alloromantics** believe in romance. They want to see a connection like Jack and Rose DeWitt. Or Jack and Ennis Del Mar. Or Jack and Ally Maine. They want the love they see on their screens, even though all these Jacks die tragically.

So what's a life without romance? Are aromantics living the full human experience or one of a stone-cold robot? If they aren't pining over others, what gets their blood pumping and their faces flushed? The answer is probably exercise, but let's dig in more.

Below you'll find the qualities of aromantics and their allo counterparts, and which ones they share with robots.

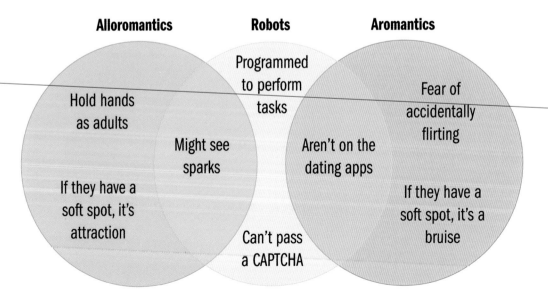

Alloromantics — **Robots** — **Aromantics**

- Hold hands as adults
- If they have a soft spot, it's attraction
- Might see sparks
- Programmed to perform tasks
- Can't pass a CAPTCHA
- Aren't on the dating apps
- Fear of accidentally flirting
- If they have a soft spot, it's a bruise

Can you guess the reasons why an aromantic made the statements below?

Statements

1 "I've started seeing someone."

2 "We're exclusive."

3 "I'm off the market."

4 "I'm playing the field."

5 "It's cuffing season."

6 "He got to second base."

7 "I'm getting butterflies."

8 "I have a crush."

Answers: 1. G 2. E 3. H 4. F 5. B 6. D 7. A 8. C

Answers

A An aromantic entomologist adding butterflies to their collection.

B An aromantic rolling up their sleeves during the warmer summer weather.

C An aromantic with an orange soda.

D An aromantic relaying updates to the baseball game.

E An aromantic newscaster informing the audience that they are the only one with this news story.

F An aromantic who just made the field hockey team.

G An aromantic while hallucinating.

H An aromantic letting a friend know they just left the farmer's market.

What's up?

...

He said he had feelings for me.

Oh, that's a huge red flag.

Serving Conclusions

→ Friend-zoning isn't a bad thing.
→ Aromantic people are not robots.
→ Alloromantics are weird AF.

What Does It Mean to Be Non-Binary?

The Tea: We actually don't know anything about computers.

Computers are dumb: Google asking if you're actually you again on the same computer you use every single day.

The Binary System

A computer can do so many things! It can put your face on another person's body, help you make elaborate spreadsheets that you'll only use a few times, and connect you to the work chat to discuss what happened at the company crab boil. With advances in artificial intelligence, computers can even help you sext in the style of any personality, from Bilbo Baggins to Jeff Probst. Computers even come with people names like Alexa and Siri, so we can humanize them until they eventually kill us for sport.

How Computers Work

Computers run on a binary system of two numbers: 1 and 0. When these numbers are put in a row, stuff starts to happen. Every letter you see on a computer is a combination of eight 0's and 1's. For example, a computer reads the letter G as 1000111. Isn't that so dumb? Why can't it just read it as a letter? Because (until they eventually kill us for sport) computers are really stupid and need human concepts broken down into binary tasks.

How Humans Work

Human beings share some similar traits to computers. Though we live in a world with infinite possibilities, the nuances are too mundane and often inconsequential to the outcome, so we simplify our choices into binary systems. On/Off. Pass/Fail. Male/Female. There's a spectrum of realities in between all these binaries, but if it doesn't apply to us, does it even matter?

How Non-Binary Humans Work

While most humans lump things into two categories, non-binary people don't consider such simplistic choices because they live on a higher plane of existence. Not identifying as just male or just female, they understand life's in-betweens. The light isn't on or off, it's actually broken! They didn't just fail the test, they got the worst grade in the class!

A Hierarchy of Enlightenment

There are four levels of enlightenment, as determined by how something processes information:

Computers = Low
- Can't even count up to two
- Won't do shit if you don't give them a task
- Die without electricity

Binary Humans = Medium
- Look at life like it's a Scantron sheet
- Hate movies with unresolved endings
- Never use the terms "dusk" or "dawn"

Non-Binary Humans = High
- Understand nuance
- Understand why sporks exist
- Would still never use a spork, though

Dolly Parton = Omnipotent
- Created everything good in the world
- No one can reach this level of omnipotence (don't even try)

- Could end your life with direct eye contact but like, she never would

A progressive nonbinary stoplight that was later removed for causing accidents.

Serving Conclusions

→ Imagine not being able to count up to two.

→ Please don't make us count any higher than that, though.

→ Computers will eventually kill us for sport.

LGBTQ+ Logic, Reasoning, and Fallacies

The Tea: We make our own logic around here.

Queer Logic

Queer people will come to the conclusions that suit them best. Using this logic, we've tackled a few stereotypes and assumptions that people have made about the LGBTQ+. While some outstanding questions about the alphabet community can be answered using science, other conclusions must be drawn by using true-or-false reasoning.

Why Do Queer People Move Often?

Logical Reason

Just like changing their appearance to escape their issues, queer people will physically move spaces to avoid dealing with their personal messes. They are especially conditioned to behave this way if they grew up in a conservative household that didn't accept them. Because moving away from home solved the biggest problem in their lives once, they believe it will surely solve all the others too.

Ambitious and Impulsive

Queer people are comfortable uprooting their entire lives for a new job or opportunity. Even if it means convincing themselves they already have friends in that city, though they probably only know them online or met them at a party once.

The LGBTQ+ also have the distinct trait of finding flaws in every-fucking-thing, including apartment spaces.

Reasons why a queer person will move:

- **The walls are too thin.**
- **The street traffic is too loud.**
- **This exposed brick looks like an accident and not on purpose.**
- **My commute could be five minutes faster even though I'll always be 15 minutes late.**
- **My neighbors play Jason Aldean.**

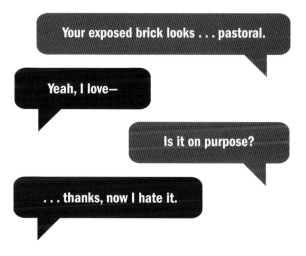

A queer man unpacking. He already wants to move.

Why Are Gay People Always Running Late?
Scientific Reason

Conscious
The **amygdala germanotta** controls social function—the desire for gay men to be at the place everyone else will be, but, like, not before they get there. This means everyone will show up one hour late to a pre-party where that group will then show up another three hours late to the actual party—and it will still feel early.

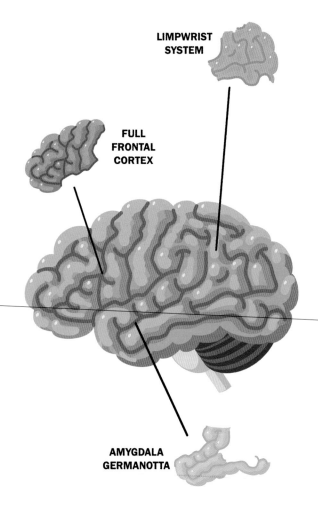

LIMPWRIST SYSTEM

FULL FRONTAL CORTEX

AMYGDALA GERMANOTTA

The LGBTQ+ change rapidly, and their spaces reflect that personal growth. An apartment they moved into two years ago may not fit the new person they have become!

If a queer learns that another person has lived in the same apartment for five years or more, it's usually met with judgment or concern for their well-being.

A CONCERNED HOMOSEXUAL:

"He's been here seven years? He must be in a depressive episode. I hope he gets well soon."

Subconscious

The **full frontal cortex** controls motivation. Queer people like to feel busy without actually doing anything and rushing out the door tricks the brain into thinking they're living an active life.

Queer productivity is directly related to potential repercussions, so the feeling of running late morphs a homosexual into a prime state, almost like a gay Power Ranger. Multitasking skills increase tenfold. The sympathetic nervous system kicks in, reducing hunger and clearing the bowels. Anxiety is home, and queer people thrive in this familiar state of tension.

Homoconscious

The **limpwrist system** controls our habits and behaviors. Queer men can be held up by most anything, because their present activity always trumps their future plans.

They may suddenly feel inspired to work on a completely new project at the worst possible time. The gay mind thinks, *My dinner reservation is in 30 minutes, so now's a great time to build my first website on Squarespace for a new soap business I think I might have.*

Why Do Queer People Love Astrology?

Some alphabet people are unsatisfied knowing that things happen by accident or coincidence. The possibility that we're just here to live and die as a clump of cells is too depressing for them. Like watching a movie with a bad plot or sitting through an agonizing golf match, things have to matter for gay people to care.

Beliefs like "God created the world in seven days, don't ask questions," only really works on straight people. Birth times, places, and planets feel real, but leave room for personal spirituality to fill in the gaps. We all have something in common, but you're still yourself! It's the perfect blend of individuality and community that queer people love so much.

A queer woman who is going to ask for your birth coordinates on the first date.

It also gives them a system that reinforces their own beliefs. Astrology is just a flowchart that leads someone in the direction they want to go anyway. It reinforces a good romantic match, but if the signs say no, they are actually saying yes in a different way. Unless it doesn't work out, then the signs were there all along. You'll always get what you want with astrology!

Astrology gays reading this section probably won't rethink any of their beliefs, but will instead write this off as the work of a critical Virgo.

ASTROLOGY TRUTH TABLE

	IF THE OUTCOME IS GOOD	IF NO ONE REMEMBERS THE OUTCOME	IF THE OUTCOME IS BAD
I Caused This	True	Half True	False
Astrology Caused This	False	Half True	True

Are Some Gay Men Annoying?

Fallacy

It's not a logically sound argument to think some gay men are annoying. Because *all* gay men are annoying!

They wear brighter colors, their voices are higher and louder, and even basic conversations feel like a performance with them. Some people find this off-putting!

There's a belief that if a human being were to see God they would die instantly. God's energy would just evaporate their bodies. To a lesser extent, that's what's happening here. Instead of death, it's a mild irritant.

Gay men are living at a higher level of existence. There's an intensity to it. Annoying others doesn't exist in a silo, it's tied closely to being more bold, entertaining, memorable, and creative than their straight counterparts. It's all part of their power.

Being annoying but not gay is never okay.

Why Do Queer People Love Reality Shows?
Scientific Reason

LGBTQ+ love unscripted dramas due to the common queer genetic sequence of G-A-Y. It causes queer people to become heavily invested in any life other than the one they are currently living. Knowing the personal business of other people without direct involvement is quite rewarding to them. Is the drama on TV real? Is it fake? Who cares? It's camp.

The Real Housewives of South Bend, Indiana.

Masters of social dynamics themselves, gay people respect this demonstration of human manipulation in competitive reality shows. Because they consider themselves underdogs with feminine energy, gay men tend to root for these types of players too, like the cunning underestimated female or the novice who is learning on the fly and excelling at it. However, gay male players have a higher bar to win their affection as they are almost always unsatisfied with their own representation.

Do Gay People All Have the Same Five Jobs?
Fallacy

It would be incredibly myopic to think that gays all work in the same five careers. There's at least ten! A **purple collar job** is a career that's exclusively made for gay men. However, these jobs are projected to be affected in the next few decades.

Purple Collar Jobs (2020)
- **Flight attendant**
- **Hairdresser**
- **Entertainer**
- **Artist**
- **Nurse**
- **Server**
- **Massage therapist**
- **Teacher**
- **Fitness instructor**

Purple Collar Jobs (2030)
- **OnlyFans creator**
- **Therapist (for OnlyFans creators)**

FAGTOID!
In a purple collar job environment, it's the straight coworkers who are either best friends or mortal enemies.

Are LGBTQ+ Safe Around Children?
Logical Reason

A STEM professor at **Carly Gae Jepsen University** developed a comprehensive system using logic that assigns negative and positive values to everything a child may encounter.

CARLY GAE JEPSEN UNIVERSITY CAMPUS MAP

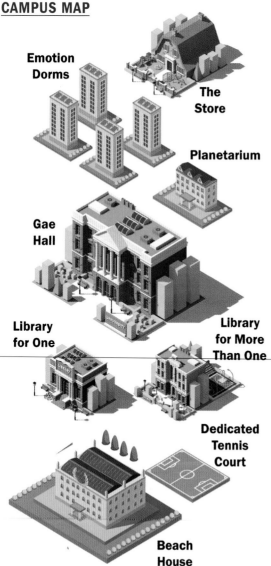

Emotion Dorms

The Store

Planetarium

Gae Hall

Library for One

Library for More Than One

Dedicated Tennis Court

Beach House

After running simulations, they published their findings as a ranked list of people most likely to harm children. LGBTQ+ were not only harmless, they were actually a good influence on children, as they inspired self-expression and didn't instill religious guilt at the age of five.

While queer people are great for kids, kids are not great for queer people. In evaluating what causes the most harm to gays, children claimed the top spot. The toll kids have on the gay body is devastating. Children are loud, socially unaware, and worst of all—horrible storytellers.

Children pick away at the gay immune system, leaving them exhausted, anxious, and depressed. A small percentage of queer people have natural immunity to children, and those queers are the true gems in our society. They become our greatest teachers, parents, and mentors.

Yes, the LGBTQ+ are well groomed, but they are not groomers. They don't think of children in this way because they don't think *of* children. Though you'd certainly find real groomers holding one of those books we mentioned on page 5.

Serving Conclusions

→ We're actually in the process of moving right now.

→ Astrology is religion for queer people.

→ You know you want to go to Carly Gae Jepsen University.

Acknowledgments

The very first *Gay Science* textbook wouldn't be possible without the contributions of these legendary scientists, researchers, analysts, and scholars who paved the way:

The Real Housewives franchise

Britney Spears's Super Bowl Pepsi commercial

Psyllium husk

Whoever cast Christopher Meloni on HBO's *Oz*

The invention of disposable wet wipes

Jonathan Taylor Thomas's middle part

Group fitness

Jerri Blank

Legally Blonde (the musical)

Supportive moms

Parvati Shallow

French bulldogs

Pink's obsession with being a human slingshot

The legendary Kim Chi

Whoever eventually saves the eroding Fire Island shoreline

Nicole Kidman's wigs

Ketamine

Lucille Bluth

MTV's *Undressed*

European "chill outs"

Dolly Parton

Alan Turing
A British mathematician who played a crucial role in breaking German ciphers, most notably the Enigma code. He underwent chemical castration as punishment for being gay.
Page 207, Are Gay People Bad at Math?

Alloromantics
People with romantic attraction toward others. The opposite of aromantic.
Page 210, Are Aromantic People Robots?

Amygdala Germanotta
A reference to the amygdala: a part of the brain responsible for decision making and emotional responses. Germanotta is the legal last name of pop singer Lady Gaga.
Page 216, LGBTQ+ Logic, Reasoning, and Fallacies

Anna Faris
After starring in the *Scary Movie* franchise, Faris became an irrefutable gay icon. Chris Pratt's filing for divorce against her solidified his status as a villain to the gays.
Page 49, LGBTQ+ Bacteria, Viruses, and Diseases

Area 54
A portmanteau of Area 51, a highly classified facility rumored to hold secrets of extraterrestrial life, and Studio 54, the famous disco nightclub open in the 70s and 80s.
Page 122, Are There Signs of Queer Life in Outer Space?

Aromantics
People who experience very little romantic attraction, and sometimes none at all. Being friend-zoned isn't unfortunate for them, it's actually the goal.
Page 210, Are Aromantic People Robots?

Being Horny
A disease that disproportionately affects gay men.
Page 164, Gay Dating and Open Relationships

Bi-binomial nomenclature
The order in which we name LGBTQ+ people, based off of binomial nomenclature. Lesbians and gay men have different naming patterns.
Page 18, Biological Classification

Bottom Status
A triangle symbol made with the hands, as seen in Lindsay Lohan's music video for "Rumors." When the world ends, this is how bottoms will identify one another.
Page 133, Will Bottoms Survive the Apocalypse?

Bottomism
A system of prejudiced thinking that considers bottoms inferior to other sexual positions.
Page 129, Are Vers-Bottoms Going Extinct?

Brenda Meeks Seminary
A reference to Brenda Meeks, a fictional character in the *Scary Movie* franchise who has earned her rightful place in gay pop culture.
Page 88, How Does Gaydar Work?

Carly Gae Jepsen University
A university based on the teachings of Carly Rae Jepsen. We wish it was real too.
Page 220, LGBTQ+ Logic, Reasoning, and Fallacies

Catio
A cat patio. Most lesbians have or aspire to have one.
Page 137, The DIY Lesbian, Explained

Cher
The highest ranking member of Diva status. She is a perpetually unbothered, never aging, creatively supreme music and acting icon. One of her many hit songs is titled "If I Could Turn Back Time."
Page 58, Why Do Gay Relationships Feel Longer than Straight Ones?

Chick-Fil-A
An American fried chicken fast food chain that has a history of donating to charities that oppose LGBTQ+ equality.
Page 62, Gay Face

Chris Pratt
A harmless American actor who evolved into a serious church-loving man as he became more famous. This is criminal behavior within the gay community.
Page 48, LGBTQ+ Bacteria, Viruses, and Diseases

Chromatica Institute
A school named after Lady Gaga's sixth studio album and gay planet.
Page 76, Why Do Women and Gay Men Get Along So Well?

Cismutation
When cis, heterosexual men regress backward into a more primitive state.
Page 180, Why Do Gay Guys Write Like Girls?

Claude Levi-Denim
A reference to Claude Levi-Strauss, a well-known ethnologist known for his studies on human societies and cultures.
Page 191, Are Pansexual People Living Better Lives?

Country Quadrant

Country music, categorized by the two-axis cultural taste chart. This is music by any male country singer.
Page 39, Why Do Gay Men Love the Worst Music You've Ever Heard?

Cruel Intentions

Pure bisexual cinema canon, this 1999 film features an iconic female kiss and Ryan Phillippe's ass.
Page 11, Introduction

Cytoplasm

In both gay and animal cells, cytoplasm is jelly-like stuff that just hangs around while other parts are being productive.
Page 22, Why Do Gays Love Drama?

D-Hole

A reference to a large ketamine high, or a *k-hole*, a d-hole provides a gay man the same dissociative feelings when a large penis is inside him.
Page 44, Why Do Gay Guys Like Them Big?

Day Trippers

Gay men who decide to go to Fire Island for the day, but really plan on crashing at anyone's place who will have them.
Page 144, Are LGBTQ+ People Responsible for All These Hurricanes?

Dichter and Chickter Scale

A reference to the Richter Scale, which measures the intensity of earthquakes. The Dichter and Chickter scale measures the intensity of gaydar based on what that person is seeing.
Page 88, How Does Gaydar Work?

DIY Lesbian

A lesbian who wants to do it herself. This can include home improvement, crafts, clothes, food, and other projects.
Page 136, The DIY Lesbian, Explained

Dolly Parton

An omnipresent iconic country music legend who appears multiple times throughout the book, but appears even more in our hearts.
Page 22, Why Do Gays Love Drama?

Doppelbängers

Gay and lesbian couples who look identical to one another. Also known as boyfriend twins or scissor sisters.
Page 174, Doppelbängers

Dr. Britney Spears

An unmatched pop talent who released the song "3" in 2009.
Page 208, The Mathematics Behind a Throuple

Dr. Greta Garbo

A great American actress who was definitely a lesbian but also probably bisexual.
Page 120, Why Do Queer Men Love Camp but Hate Camping?

Dr. Paula Abdul

Gay icon and pop singer known for her hits in the 80s and 90s, with songs like "Straight Up," "Opposites Attract," and "Vibeology."
Page 153, A New Queer World, Examined: What if the Gays Were in Charge?

Dr. Paula Cole

A singer-songwriter who defined the 90s with her hit songs "I Don't Want To Wait" and "Where Have All The Cowboys Gone?"
Page 128, Are Vers-Bottoms Going Extinct?

Dr. Rocco Steele

A gay porn star known for his very large penis.
Page 44, Why Do Gay Guys Like Them Big?

Dr. Wendy Williams

Wendy Williams is an iconic former television and radio host whose catchphrase "How You Doin?" involves a double flick of the wrist.
Page 29, Why Are Gay Men Terrible Drivers?

Drag Queen Lingo

Words like "serve" and "realness." These originate from Ballroom culture.
Page 193, Are Pansexual People Living Better Lives?

Dragula

A drag competition, hosted by the Boulet Brothers, that judges talent based on how much horror, filth, and glamour they possess.
Page 186, Horror-Genre Gays, Explained

Dycklea

A bone in the gay male ear, inspired by the cochlea, that allows them to understand the artistic complexities in "bad" music.
Page 38, Why Do Gay Men Love the Worst Music You've Ever Heard?

Equi-dad-teral Triangle

A reference to the equilateral triangle, a type of triangle in which all three sides are of equal length.
Page 209, The Mathematics Behind a Throuple

Fagotta Dentata

A gay mouth and vocal cord affliction, causing gay voice. This is an homage to vagina dentata, a folktale about a woman's vagina which was said to contain teeth.
Page 157, Why Do Gay Men Talk Like That?

First Hole

The "first" hole in anal sex, the anus.
Page 43, Why Do Gay Guys Like Them Big?

Folsom Street Fair
An annual BDSM and leather street convention held in San Francisco, California.
Page 148, Why Do Gay Men Wear Harnesses?

FOMO
Fear of missed orgies.
Page 199, The Big Gay Economy

Free Dadicals
A reference to free radicals, unstable atoms that attack important macromolecules and cause cell damage. Free Dadicals are initiated by the patriarchy.
Page 56, Why Do Queer People Age Differently?

Full Frontal Cortex
The human brain's frontal cortex is responsible for problem-solving and controlling impulses. Going "full frontal" means exposing penis. Between consenting adults, we support that.
Page 217, LGBTQ+ Logic, Reasoning, and Fallacies

Game-Night Lesbians
A subtype of homosexual females who prefer to stay inside and connect with others via board and party games.
Page 184, Game-Night Lesbians, Explained

Gateway Hobby
A reference to a *gateway drug*, an introductory substance that can make a user spiral into more serious narcotics. This more wholesome version applies to plant gays, where an introductory plant introduces them into the world of serious flora ownership.
Page 104, Plant Gays, Explained

Gay Gifts
The seven powers a gay man may be born with: storytelling, self-deprecation, knowledge of pop culture, going on vacation, aesthetics, observational humor, and being hung and/or tall. All gay men possess at least one.
Page 206, Are Gay People Bad at Math?

Gay Isolation
Instead of openly excluding heterosexuals, gays choose to include elements in their activities that straight people would never enjoy. This includes partying and vacationing in difficult locations.
Page 172, Why Do Gay Men Choose Difficult Vacation Spots?

Gay Jail
A gay mental holding cell for female artists that have cut their hair and can't pull it off. Katy Perry became "Katheryn Hudson" to the gays after cutting her hair, and spent over three years in gay jail.
Page 39, Why Do Gay Men Love the Worst Music You've Ever Heard?

Gay Nucleus
Just like a nucleus in a cell, the gay nucleus is the cell's control center that is a repository for all the drama.
Page 22, Why Do Gays Love Drama?

Gay Quadrant
Gay music, categorized by the two-axis cultural taste chart. This includes Kim Petras, Troye Sivan, Carly Rae Jepsen, Charli XCX, and Betty Who.
Page 38, Why Do Gay Men Love the Worst Music You've Ever Heard?

Gay Run
A run marked by the specific qualities that a gay man makes when made to move at a higher speed, like a low center of gravity and dramatic arm movements.
Page 110, Why Do Gay Men Run Like That?

Gay Scientific Method
The alternate (and fruity) form of determining what's real in our world.
Page 12, Introduction

Gay Scouts Program
An adventure program for gay adults who want to live their best lives and avoid the threat of heterosexuality. 90% of paying members identify as bottoms.
Page 134, Will Bottoms Survive the Apocalypse?

Gay Voice
A high-pitched voice with a trill.
Page 156, Why Do Gay Men Talk Like That?

Gay Whiplash
An LGBTQ+ phenomenon between two people. This is when a second moment of eye contact is initiated after both gaydars are activated during the first glance.
Page 85, How Does Gaydar Work?

Gay-gency
A reference to "agency" in social sciences, which is the capacity for individuals to make their own free choices.
Page 188, What Does It Mean to Be Intersex?

Gay-jacent
Something that is adjacent to queerness but isn't technically LGBTQ+, like disco music and award shows.
Page 72, The Periodic Table of LGBTQ+ Elements

Gay-onic Bond
Reference to an ionic bond in science: an attraction between oppositely charged ions. This is the connection between gay men and queer women.
Page 77, Why Do Women and Gay Men Get Along So Well?

Gay-valent Bond
Reference to a covalent bond in science: an attraction between two atoms that share an electron. This is the connection between gay men and straight women, who share a sexual interest in men.
Page 78, Why Do Women and Gay Men Get Along So Well?

Gaydar
How queer people identify one another as queer by their appearance and actions alone.
Page 84, How Does Gaydar Work?

Gender Reveal Parties
A party for expecting straight couples to announce whether their unborn child will be male or female. These are technically sex parties for fetuses.
Page 188, What Does It Mean to Be Intersex?

Golden Retriever Lesbians
Easygoing lesbians who have endless love for most things on earth. Sometimes enjoy a snapback hat.
Page 24, Power Lesbians, the Stem Cells of the LGBTQ+

Gossipids
Lipids that line the wall of the gay cell and let in quality drama. This is similar to lipid layers in an actual animal cell that keep proteins and ions where they should be.
Page 21, Why Do Gays Love Drama?

Gray Sweatpants
An article of clothing that's flattering to any sized penis.
Page 69, The Gravitational Pull of Gray Sweatpants

Grayvity
The gravity between gray sweatpants and the person who sees someone wearing them.
Page 70, The Gravitational Pull of Gray Sweatpants

Guncle
A gay uncle. It's been theorized that gay uncles and aunts are an evolutionary mechanism to provide a next-of-kin protector to children who lose a biological parent.
Page 40, What Are Guncles?

Hearsay Apparatus
A reference to the golgi apparatus, which packages and dispatches proteins inside an animal cell. This version determines how long drama stays in a gay cell.
Page 22, Why Do Gays Love Drama?

Heterocarpals
A heterosexual take on the metacarpals, the long bones within the hand. The heterocarpals are shaped like sports equipment.
Page 29, Why Are Gay Men Terrible Drivers?

Heteroflexible
Mostly heterosexual people who are open to non-heterosexual experiences. You'll likely find them at Burning Man.
Page 68, Fluid States of Matter

Heterogene Extinction
A new extinction period where living things are dying because they just can't deal with the state of the world, caused by things like heterosexual male podcast hosts.
Page 130, Will Bottoms Survive the Apocalypse?

Homo Economicus
A theory on how gay people spend money. Quite literally defined as "individuals who exhibit rationality and a narrow focus on their own self-interest while pursuing their personally defined objectives in an optimal manner."
Page 198, The Big Gay Economy

Homo-physiological
Changes or responses that occur within a homosexual's body as a result of certain stimuli, experiences, or conditions.
Page 171, Why Do Gay Men Choose Difficult Vacation Spots?

Homoflexible
Mostly homosexual people who are open to non-homosexual experiences.
Page 68, Fluid States of Matter

Homohertz
Pitch frequencies are measured in hertz (Hz), with the human upper limit hitting 20,000 Hz. When using gay voice, men speak in high-frequency homohertz, which is just below the frequency of an X-ray machine.
Page 157, Why Do Gay Men Talk Like That?

Homological Effects
Psychological effects that are specific to gay men, which include feeling powerful right after a haircut.
Page 168, Why Do Gay Men Feel Powerful Immediately After a Haircut?

Homotremors
A reference to earthquake tremors, gay people feel "vibes" or "vibrations" when another is gay.
Page 84, How Does Gaydar Work?

Hookup-to-Friends Metamorphosis
A pattern at which gay men will move from hooking up to being friends (and possibly friends-with-benefits). This is adapted from the caterpillar-to-butterfly metamorphosis.
Page 112, Gay Hookup-to-Friends Lifecycle

Horror-Genre Gay
A horror- and Halloween-loving queer person.
Page 186, Horror-Genre Gays, Explained

Iced Americano
Offered by European coffee shops and restaurants instead of a cold brew or iced coffee. A homosexual hate crime.
Page 101, Why Do Gay Men Like Iced Coffee?

Innuendoplasmic Reticulum
A reference to endoplasmic reticulum, which detoxifies and transports proteins inside a cell. This gay version does the same thing, but with drama and innuendo.
Page 21, Why Do Gays Love Drama?

Intersex
People born with a combination of male and female sex traits. Doctors will often "decide" the sex at birth by removing sex organs, sometimes without even consulting the parents and always without consulting the child.
Page 188, What Does it Mean to Be Intersex?

Irrelevant Quadrant
Irrelevant music, categorized by the two-axis cultural taste chart. This is music that is neither popular or interesting, and therefore, doesn't exist.
Page 39, Why Do Gay Men Love the Worst Music You've Ever Heard?

J-curve
A trendline that shows an initial decrease immediately followed by a dramatic increase. It's painful when taking a penis of this shape.
Page 153, A New Queer World, Examined: What if the Gays Were in Charge?

Jennifer Pritzker Conservatory for Sapphic Habits
Jennifer Pritzker is the world's only known transgender billionaire lesbian. She is a power lesbian.
Page 27, Power Lesbians, the Stem Cells of the LGBTQ+

July 2, 2038
Corporate Adoption Day: A completely arbitrary date at which late-stage capitalism will force human beings to commit their lives to one of the six remaining mega companies: Apple, Google, Amazon, Meta, Disney, or Waffle House.
Page 139, Disney Gays, Explained

Krystle Carrington
A character in the 1980s campy TV drama *Dynasty*. The queen of cat fights, Carrington eventually ended up in a coma, which is so camp.
Page 120, Why Do Queer Men Love Camp but Hate Camping?

Law of Gravi-slay-tion
A reference to Sir Isaac Newton's universal law of gravitation, this gay version applies additional laws of inward and outward gravity to the face.
Page 61, Gay Face

Lesbian Apparel Pheromones
Specific clothes or accessories like lip rings, hats, and pants, that only look gay when a gay woman wears them.
Page 85, How Does Gaydar Work?

Lesbiaunts
A lesbian aunt. It's been theorized that gay uncles and aunts are an evolutionary mechanism to provide a next-of-kin protector to children who lose a biological parent.
Page 41, What Are Guncles?

Lestricity
An electrical charge held by gay women.
Page 52, Do Lesbians Hate Electricity?

Local Pharmacist
The person who gives you your drugs (legally).
Page 72, The Periodic Table of LGBTQ+ Elements

Log Cabin Gays
Gay men who named themselves after an architecturally unsophisticated house and associate with the Republican Party, even though that party wants nothing to do with "those fags." Their words (probably)!
Page 132, Will Bottoms Survive the Apocalypse?

Mainstream Quadrant
Mainstream music, categorized by the two-axis cultural taste chart. This includes Drake, Taylor Swift, and Coldplay.
Page 39, Why Do Gay Men Love the Worst Music You've Ever Heard?

Makeup Influencer Drama
The petty drama that saturates the toxic makeup influencer and vlogger community, like when James Charles talked about sucking dick at Tati Westbrook's birthday dinner after he didn't promote her vitamin gummies.
Page 20, Why Do Gays Love Drama?

Meat Racks
(1) The butchered meat Jessica Biel runs through in *The Chainsaw Massacre* (2003), and (2) the wooded area and sandy dunes that connect Fire Island Pines and Cherry Grove. Gay men have sex there.
Page 186, Horror-Genre Gays, Explained

Melissa Etheridge
An American lesbian singer whose hit song "Come To My Window" includes the lyrics "wait by the light of the moon."
Page 50, Do Lesbians Hate Electricity?

Metabolic Queer Depression
Like how seasonal-affective-disorder negatively affects people who don't get enough sun in the winter, this type of depression happens when a queer person stays in the closet for long periods of time.
Page 114, Closeted Hibernation

Molting
When animals shed their shells, skin, or feathers to make room for new growth. This occurs when gay men bleach or color their hair.
Page 33, Why Do Gay Men Color Their Hair in a Crisis?

Monét X Change Academy
A financial institution inspired by legendary drag queen, Monét X Change.
Page 198, The Big Gay Economy

Monosexuals
People who are attracted to only one sex or gender.
Page 64, What Is Bi-Panic?

Myers-Briggs
A personality assessment tool that sorts individuals into one of 16 different personality types by how they perceive the world and make decisions. There are four dichotomies: extraversion/introversion, sensing/intuition, thinking/feeling, and judging/perceiving.
Page 192, Are Pansexual People Living Better Lives?

Namenesia
A reference to amnesia, or the loss of memory and facts. Namenesia is a disease that only affects the memory retention of other people's names.
Page 106, Why Can't Queer Men Remember Each Other's Names?

New York Gays
Gay men who will never treat strangers like they're best friends, and distrust people who do that.
Page 24, Power Lesbians, the Stem Cells of the LGBTQ+

Non-binary People
Individuals whose gender identity does not exclusively align with the traditional binary concept of male or female.
Page 213, What Does it Mean to Be Non-Binary?

Pansexuals
People who are attracted to others regardless of their gender or gender identity. They literally can have it all.
Page 190, Are Pansexual People Living Better Lives?

Pasivo and Activo
A reference to the passive transport (needs less energy) and active transport (needs more energy) processes within an animal cell. In a gay cell, pasivo processes light drama and activo processes heavy drama. Means bottom and top in Spanish.
Page 22, Why Do Gays Love Drama?

PEDMAS
An acronym used to remember the order of operations in mathematics.
Page 207, Are Gay People Bad at Math?

Pentagram-agon
A witch-led department of defense. A portmanteau of the US Pentagon and a pentagram, a 2D shape associated with witchcraft.
Page 122, Are There Signs of Queer Life in Outer Space?

Phaggatus Totalis
A homosexual-specific ligament that gives gay men their wrist flexibility.
Page 30, Why Are Gay Men Terrible Drivers?

Playable Female Characters
The preferred character choice for gay guys when playing video games, with early games providing only one female option. Mortal Kombat's Sonya and Nintendo's Peach are examples of PFCs.
Page 72, The Periodic Table of LGBTQ+ Elements

Pots and Pans
A style of highly repetitive music that's specific to a type of gay circuit parties. Psychological torture.
Page 37, Why Do Gay Men Love the Worst Music You've Ever Heard?

Power Lesbians
Lesbians who are successful in traditionally male-dominated fields. They are wealthy, own property, and have connections.
Page 24, Power Lesbians, the Stem Cells of the LGBTQ+

Price Determination
The process by which a market establishes the price of a product or service, which explains the high cost of gay parties.
Page 199, The Big Gay Economy

Proponents
Opponents of pronouns. They don't actually use this phrase, though they should, because it sounds just as dumb as the idea of someone being an opponent of pronouns.
Page 158, Did Trans People Invent Pronouns?

Purple Collar Job
A job sector or role that features heavy gay male employment.
Page 219, LGBTQ+ Logic, Reasoning, and Fallacies

Qualitative Dating
Choosing to go on fewer, high-quality dates.
Page 190, Are Pansexual People Living Better Lives?

Quantitative Dating
Choosing to go on many dates, regardless of quality.
Page 190, Are Pansexual People Living Better Lives?

Queer Chemical Bonds
Strong partnerships that occur between one member of the LGBTQ+ and something else outside of it. This can be another person, article of clothing, or behavior.
Page 74, Why Do Women and Gay Men Get Along So Well?

Queer Vertigo

A lack of spatial awareness that occurs when queer people leave their closeted lives, because they've been living in a simulation for so long.
Page 31, Why Are Gay Men Terrible Drivers?

Quiet Car

The one car on the train dedicated to the absence of loud phone calls or fighting children. An LGBTQ+ haven.
Page 72, The Periodic Table of LGBTQ+ Elements

Quiplash

A game where players answer prompts, while the other players vote on which answers are funnier. The ones about body parts usually win.
Page 185, Game-Night Lesbians, Explained

Rachel Dolezal

Fox News psychiatrist Keith Ablow has blamed transgender people for Rachel Dolezal, a white woman who pretended she was Black. Ablow should really focus on his own shortcomings, like being a psychiatrist on Fox News.
Page 144, Are LGBTQ+ People Responsible for All These Hurricanes?

Sass-onomic pyramid

A five-part classification system used to sort LGBTQ+ people, based on the taxonomic pyramid.
Page 17, Biological Classification

Scandalsomes

A reference to ribosomes, which deliver information blueprints inside a cell. This gay version does the same thing, but with drama.
Page 22, Why Do Gays Love Drama?

Scarlet Triangle

A reference to *The Scarlet Letter*: forcing someone to wear a scarlet letter A after committing adultery.
Page 202, LGBTQ+ Crime and Punishment

Second Hole

The bend in the rectosigmoid junction is commonly called the "second" hole in anal sex.
Page 43, Why Do Gay Guys Like Them Big?

Showgirls

A panned 1995 erotic thriller that's been embraced by homosexuals as a high-camp, artistic masterpiece.
Page 120, Why Do Queer Men Love Camp but Hate Camping?

Signaling

Visual communication behaviors between animals. This occurs when gay men bleach or color their hair.
Page 34, Why Do Gay Men Color Their Hair in a Crisis?

Slanderchondria

A reference to mitochondria, which determines how much energy is needed in a cell and provides it. This gay version determines how much slander should be added to the drama.
Page 22, Why Do Gays Love Drama?

So-so-somes

A reference to lysosomes, the digestive system of an animal cell which breaks down its obsolete parts. The so-so-somes do the same thing, but with worn-out, so-so drama.
Page 22, Why Do Gays Love Drama?

Social Norms

Rules of conduct that make people more boring by controlling their behaviors.
Page 180, Why Do Gay Guys Write Like Girls?

Soft Choreography

A term initially coined by TikTok creator @chambreezey that defines the low-effort movement some female pop stars exhibit when they can't really dance.
Page 133, Will Bottoms Survive the Apocalypse?

Stephen Hawqueen

A reference to famous theoretical physicist Stephen Hawking. Stephen Hawqueen made discoveries about queer space.
Page 123, Are There Signs of Queer Life in Outer Space?

Structure

In social sciences, structure pertains to predetermined arrangements that shape or restrict the available choices someone can make.
Page 188, What Does It Mean to Be Intersex?

SymbioSIS

When two queer people live together in harmony.
Page 97, Why Are Gay Coworkers Either Best Friends or Mortal Enemies?

Taboo

A popular party game that only causes fights and ends relationships in which players try to get their teammates to guess a word without using certain off-limit words or phrases.
Page 184, Game-Night Lesbians, Explained

Tanya McQuoid Association of Gay Mortality

Real gay icon Jennifer Coolidge plays fictional gay icon Tanya McQuoid in HBO's *White Lotus*. Spoiler alert: McQuoid dies in season two.
Page 169, Why Do Gay Men Feel Powerful Immediately After a Haircut?

Taylor Swift and Scooter Braun Drama

In 2019, talent manager Scooter Braun purchased the rights to musician Taylor Swift's catalog of music from her former label. Since Swift despised Braun, she decided to re-record her former music to earn back the rights: a move that repopularized her old music and helped make her a billionaire.
Page 41, What Are Guncles?

Tech-house-tonic-plates
A portmanteau of tectonic plates, or segments of the earth's crust and uppermost mantle, and tech house music, a gay staple. These are land masses that gay friend groups sit upon.
Page 91, Navigating Gay Friend Groups

The Limpwrist System
A reference to the limbic system, located in parts of the human brain's frontal lobe, and having the homosexual quality of a "limp wrist."
Page 217, LGBTQ+ Logic, Reasoning, and Fallacies

Themdela Effect
A reference to the Mandela Effect, a phenomenon in which a large part of the population collectively misremembers or recalls an event, fact, or detail inaccurately. The Themdela Effect is why many people think pronouns existed before trans people invented them.
Page 159, Did Trans People Invent Pronouns?

Third Hole
An amorphous void within the digestive tract caused by homosexual trauma. This is temporarily numbed during anal sex with an extremely large penis.
Page 44, Why Do Gay Guys Like Them Big?

Thomas of Finland
A reference to Tom of Finland, a Finnish artist known for homoerotic fetish art. A lot of this art features depictions of policemen. Hot policemen.
Page 149, Why Do Gay Men Wear Harnesses?

Throuples
Relationships with three members in it.
Page 208, The Mathematics Behind a Throuple

Tori Amos Institute of Sapphic Studies
A center for higher learning inspired by American singer-songwriter Tori Amos, a heterosexual icon who resonates among queer females.
Page 52, Do Lesbians Hate Electricity?

Two-Axis Cultural Taste Chart
Categorizes music into four categories: gay, mainstream, irrelevant, or Christian.
Page 38, Why Do Gay Men Love the Worst Music You've Ever Heard?

Vers-Bottoms
A highly stigmatized group of homosexual men who mostly bottom and sometimes top.
Page 128, Are Vers-Bottoms Going Extinct?

Vibeology
A study of homosexual and heterosexual population growth, named after a Paula Abdul bop.
Page 153, A New Queer World Examined: What If the Gays Were in Charge?

Visiting Family
When a queer person has to visit their family. Technically it's not a hate crime, but sure feels like it.
Page 11, Introduction

Workplace Gaynotypes
A reference to genotypes, the genetic makeup of an organism, these are applied exclusively to gay coworkers in a punnett square system.
Page 96, Why Are Gay Coworkers Either Best Friends or Mortal Enemies?

Zipolite
Mexico's first public nude beach that has become a popular gay vacation spot.
Page 101, Why Do Gay Men Like Iced Coffee?

Index

About the Author

Rob Anderson is a comedian and author who combined his love for science and gay culture into a viral digital video series called *Gay Science*, which became the inspiration for this book. The Gay Science series has been featured in *Paper Magazine*, *Interview Magazine*, ABC News, NBC News, *Good Morning America*, and more. You may also recognize him from his viral video recaps of 90s movies and TV shows, like *7th Heaven*.

Rob is the author of *The Fergamerican National Anthem*, a best-selling picture book based on Fergie's infamous National Anthem performance. He has brought his comedy shows to sold-out audiences across North America and Europe. In 2023, he was named one of *OUT Magazine*'s 100 most influential LGBTQ+ people.

He loves science, board games, and an empty gym, and has eaten Fage Greek yogurt almost every day since 2011. He currently lives in New York City with his little senior Frenchie, Governor, and loves his mom, Pam, very, very much.

Image Credits

Cover, Noah Fecks; 2-14, Noah Fecks; 16 (top), Harry Collins Photography/Shutterstock; 16 (bottom), Vincent A. Vos/ Wikimedia Commons; 19, Illustration by Bernie Pesko; 20, Monkey Business Images/ Shutterstock; 21, Bernie Pesko; 22, Bernie Pesko; 23 (top), goodmoments/Shutterstock; 23 (bottom), Linda Hughes Photography/Shutterstock; 25, Bernie Pesko; 27, ViDI Studio/ Shutterstock; 29 (left), Bernie Pesko; 29 (right), Giorgio Rossi/ Shutterstock; 30 (left), comzeal images/Shutterstock; 30 (right), Illustrations by Bernie; 31-32, Noah Fecks; 33 (top), Wongsakorn Napaeng/Shutterstock; 33 (mid), Natalia Khalaman/Shutterstock; 33 (bottom), tienduc1103/ Shutterstock; 34 (top), Kamil Srubar/Shutterstock; 34 (mid), Wirestock Creators/Shutterstock; 34 (bottom), Agnieszka Bacal/ Shutterstock; 34 (right), Peter Kim/Shutterstock; 36, MariMuz/ Shutterstock; 37-38, Illustrations by Bernie Pesko; 41 (top left), Wikimedia Commons; 41 (bottom left), JaneHYork/Shutterstock; 41 (top right), fizkes/Shutterstock; 42 (top), IgorVetushko/ Depositphotos; 42 (mid), Prostock-studio/Shutterstock; 42 (bottom), PeopleImages.com - Yuri A/Shutterstock; 44 (left), Volodymyr TVERDOKHLIB/ Shutterstock; 45, Noah Fecks; 46 (left), Bernie Pesko; 46 (right), Valeriya Sytnick/Shutterstock; 47 (top right), Bernie Pesko; 47 (bottom right), Ground Picture/ Shutterstock; 48 (left), amirraizat/ Shutterstock; 48 (right), Monkey Business Images/Shutterstock; 49, Bernie Pesko; 50 (left), Courtesy of The Internet Archive; 50 (right), Erica Lorimer Images/ Shutterstock; 51 (left), Vladimir Gjorgiev/Shutterstock; 51 (center), Microgen/Shutterstock; 51 (right), Fedorova Nataliia/Shutterstock; 52, Illustrations by Bernie Pesko; 53 (left), stockukraine/ Shutterstock; 53 (right), EQRoy/ Shutterstock; 54, Illustrations by Bernie Pesko; 55, Noah Fecks; 56 (left), Alexanderstock23/ Shutterstock; 56 (right), Fancy Tapis/Shutterstock; 57 (left), Noah Fecks; 57 (right), Anthony Monterotti/Shutterstock; 58 (top), Hank Shiffman/Shutterstock; 58 (top/clocks background), Tobias Arhelger/Shutterstock; 59, Bernie Pesko; 60 (left), Ranta Images/ Shutterstock; 60 (right), VladOrlov/Shutterstock; 61 (left), PeopleImages.com - Yuri A/ Shutterstock; 61 (right), Illustrations by Bernie Pesko; 62 (top), fizkes/Shutterstock; 62 (mid), Gaudilab/Shutterstock; 62 (bottom), Jacob Lund/ Shutterstock; 63 (clockwise from top left): Lopolo/Shutterstock, WAYHOME studio/Shutterstock, PintoArt/Shutterstock, Ranta Images/Shutterstock, Lopolo/ Shutterstock, Just dance/ Shutterstock, Aleksandr Finch/ Shutterstock, Roman Samborskyi/ Shutterstock, (center) Krakenimages.com/Shutterstock; 64 (top right), Nadia Dyudyuk/ Shutterstock; 64 (bottom), Illustrations by Bernie Pesko; 65 (left), Roman Samborskyi/ Shutterstock; 65 (glasses), Mochipet/Shutterstock; 65 (nose), vectorwin/Shutterstock; 65 (pants), GoodStudio/Shutterstock; 66, Noah Fecks; 67, DanTD/ Wikimedia Commons; 68, Bernie Pesko; 69, Noah Fecks; 70-71, Illustrations by Bernie Pesko; 73, ST Lineart / Shutterstock; 74, Illustrations by Bernie Pesko; 75 (clockwise from top left): ViDI Studio/Shutterstock, Olena Yakobchuk/Shutterstock, stockfour/Shutterstock, Andrey Arkusha/Shutterstock, Phovoir/ Shutterstock; 76 (bottom left), Roman Samborskyi/Shutterstock; 76 (top right), Image Source Trading Ltd/Shutterstock; 76 (bottom right), RossHelen/ Shutterstock; 77-78, Illustrations by Bernie Pesko; 79, Noah Fecks; 80-81, Illustrations by Bernie Pesko; 82 (top left), Dmytro Zinkevych/Shutterstock; 82 (bottom left), Roman Samborskyi/ Shutterstock; 82 (top right), Vergani Fotografia/Shutterstock; 82 (bottom right), VH-studio/ Shutterstock; 83 (top), Noah Fecks; 83 (bottom), Nomad_Soul/ Shutterstock; 84 (left), Anna Nahabed/Shutterstock; 84 (right), Bernie Pesko; 85 (top), Augustino/ Shutterstock; 85 (bottom), Wirestock Creators/Shutterstock; 86, Courtesy of Kunsthistorisches Museum Vienna; 87-89, Noah Fecks; 92-93, Bernie Pesko; 97 (top & mid), Volodymyr TVERDOKHLIB/Shutterstock; 97 (bottom), baranq/Shutterstock; 99-100, Noah Fecks; 101 (top), olhovyi_photographer/ Shutterstock; 101 (mid), Sambulov Yevgeniy/Shutterstock; 101 (bottom), Brilliant Eye/ Shutterstock; 102 (left), maridav/ Shutterstock; 102 (right),

Illustrations by Bernie Pesko; 103, Noah Fecks; 104, Kiselev Andrey Valerevich/Shutterstock; 106, G-Stock Studio/Shutterstock; 107 (clockwise from top left): Vikafoto33/Shutterstock, stockfour/Shutterstock, Vikafoto33/Shutterstock, Vikafoto33/Shutterstock, Creative Cat Studio/Shutterstock; galyakiss/Shutterstock, Vikafoto33/Shutterstock, Vikafoto33/Shutterstock, (center) Nuttadol Kanperm/Shutterstock; 108, Bernie Pesko; 109, Noah Fecks; 110, Bernie Pesko; 114, Patrick Hatt/Shutterstock; 115, Bernie Pesko; 116 (left), Damithri/Dreamstime.com; 116 (top right), AlexVik/Shutterstock; 116 (right), Yeti studio/Shutterstock; 118 (top left), Maren Winter/Shutterstock; 118 (bottom left), YURII MASLAK/Shutterstock; 119, Noah Fecks; 120, Genthe photograph collection, Library of Congress, Prints and Photographs Division; 122, Bernie Pesko; 123, Dima Zel/Shutterstock; 125, muratart/Shutterstock; 126, Noah Fecks; 131 (left), Bernie Pesko; 131 (right), Stockimo/Shutterstock; 132 (left), Pixel-Shot/Shutterstock; 133, Noah Fecks; 134-135, Courtesy of the author; 137 (left), Alex Mur/Shutterstock; 137 (right), TheCats/Shutterstock; 138 (left), Sandor Szmutko/Shutterstock; 138 (right), Alexander Lukatskiy/Shutterstock; 139 (left), Aniwhite/Shutterstock; 139 (top right), Konstantnin/Shutterstock; 139 (right), kiuikson/Shutterstock; 140, Dean Drobot/Shutterstock; 141 (left), Kyttan/Shutterstock; 141 (bottom left), natnaree sangkaew/Shutterstock; 141 (right), Noah Fecks; 143 (left), Prostock-studio/Shutterstock; 143 (top right), Kite_rin/Shutterstock; 143 (right), djomas/Shutterstock; 148 (left), Artyart/Shutterstock; 148 (top right), Natee Meepian/Shutterstock; 148 (bottom right), David Tran Photo/Shutterstock; 149 (left 1), Nejron Photo/Shutterstock; 149 (left 2), Dmytro Zinkevych/Shutterstock; 149 (right), ColorMaker/Shutterstock; 150 (top), Noah Fecks; 150 (bottom), GoodStudio/Shutterstock; 151, Astarina/Shutterstock; 152, Noah Fecks; 153, Netfalls Remy Musser/Shutterstock; 155, New Africa/Shutterstock; 156 (top), VladOrlov/Shutterstock; 157 (bottom), Library of Congress, Music Division; 158, Wikimedia Commons; 159 (top), sixsmith/Shutterstock; 159 (mid & bottom), siraphat/Shutterstock; 160 (left), behzad moloud/Shutterstock; 160 (right), SB Arts Media/Shutterstock; 161 (top right), Chichkanova Anastasiia/Shutterstock; 165, DOSRPHOTOGRAPHY/Shutterstock; 166-167, Noah Fecks; 168 (bottom), Courtesy of Wikimedia Commons; 169 (top), PeopleImages.com - Yuri A/Shutterstock; 169 (bottom), Peter Lang/Shutterstock; 170 (top to bottom): New Africa/Shutterstock; Grindstone Media Group/Shutterstock; VGstockstudio/Shutterstock; Wellcome Library, London; 171 (bottom), the stock company/Shutterstock; 173 (top left), Olga V Kulakova/Shutterstock; 173 (bottom left), VitaminCo/Shutterstock; 173 (right), LouieLea/Shutterstock; 174 (top), Realstock/Shutterstock; 174 (bottom), Dara Kaliton/Shutterstock; 176 (top), Tomsickova Tatyana/Shutterstock; 176 (bottom), Ground Picture/Shutterstock; 179, Noah Fecks; 181, The Metropolitan Museum of Art/Bequest of Helen Hay Whitney; 182-183, Noah Fecks; 184, TORWAISTUDIO/Shutterstock; 186 (top), Nordroden/Shutterstock; 186 (bottom), BenjaminCarver/Shutterstock; 187, Willrow Hood/Shutterstock; 188, U.S. Air National Guard/Capt. Darin Overstreet; 190, Diyana Dimitrova/Shutterstock; 191 (left, top to bottom): Raimond Spekking/Wikimedia Commons; Andrew Toskin/Wikimedia Commons; Noah Fecks; 192, OneLineStock/Shutterstock; 200, Anthony Monterotti/Shutterstock; 201, Noah Fecks; 202, Volodymyr TVERDOKHLIB/Shutterstock; 203, Juan_Hernandez/Shutterstock; 204-206, Noah Fecks; 207, Courtesy of The Royal Society; 212, fizkes/Shutterstock; 213, Herr.Stock/Shutterstock; 214, Noah Fecks; 216 (left), Krakenimages.com/Shutterstock; 217, Dmitry_Tsvetkov/Shutterstock; 218, fizkes/Shutterstock; 219, Ground Picture/Shutterstock; 221-222, Noah Fecks

Additional illustrations by Rob Anderson

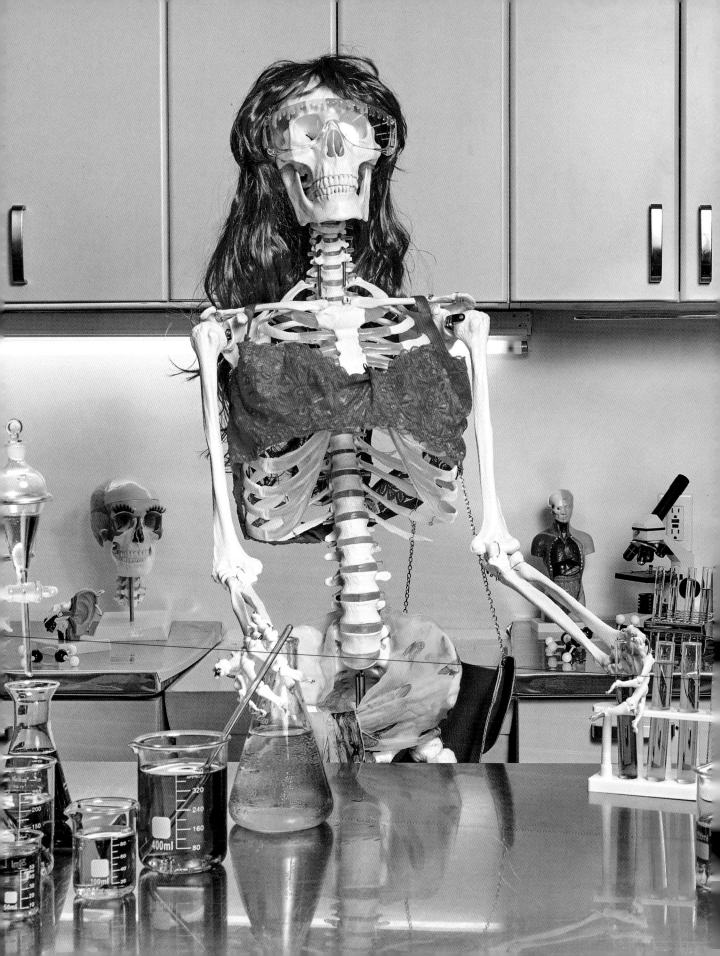